REWIRE

YOUR **BRAIN**

Develop MENTAL Flexibility, Change HABITS, Stop PROCRASTINATION and Alter MEMORIES Based on NEUROSCIENCE RESEARCH

By

LYNN GREEN

Copyright © 2021 LYNN GREEN All rights reserved.

No part of this guide may be reproduced in any form without permission in writing from the publisher except in the case of brief quotations embodied in critical chapters or reviews.

Legal & Disclaimer

The information contained in this book and its contents is not designed to replace or take the place of any form of medical or professional advice; and is not meant to replace the need for independent medical, financial, legal or other professional advice or services, as may be required. The content and information in this book have been provided for educational and entertainment purposes only.

The content and information contained in this book has been compiled from sources deemed reliable, and it is accurate to the best of the Author's knowledge, information and belief. However, the Author cannot guarantee its accuracy and validity and cannot be held liable for any errors and/or omissions. Further, changes are periodically made to this book as and when needed. Where appropriate and/or necessary, you must consult a professional (including but not limited to your doctor, attorney, financial advisor or such other professional advisor) before using any of the suggested remedies, techniques, or information in this book.

Upon using the contents and information contained in this book, you agree to hold harmless the Author from and against any damages, costs, and expenses, including any legal fees potentially resulting from the application of any of the information provided by this book. This disclaimer applies to any loss, damages or injury caused by the use and application, whether directly or indirectly, of any advice or information presented, whether for breach of contract, tort, negligence, personal injury, criminal intent, or under any other cause of action.

You agree to accept all risks of using the information presented inside this book.

You agree that by continuing to read this book, where appropriate and/or necessary, you shall consult a professional (including but not limited to your doctor, attorney, or financial advisor or such other advisor as needed) before using any of the suggested remedies, techniques, or information in this book.

CONTENTS

How to Reconnect Your Burned Brain: Advice from A Neurologist

You might be surprised, but your brain often plays against you. Everyone in life has moments of anxiety and difficult times. We could experience them in a much calmer and more productive way if this clump of neurons didn't "put sticks in the wheel". The good news is: you can learn how to reconfigure your brain. It is not difficult.

The burnout interventions I am about to suggest are probably the ones you already know. The problem is that when it comes to adding another activity to your schedule, past experiences may have left you with the expectation that there wasn't enough time - or you've tried things like this before and haven't noticed any changes. So, you stopped.

My belief is that when you understand what happened in your brain to build the hopelessness and frustration of burnout, you will connect with the logic of the interventions. Then, with the addition of the video game model to increase the neurochemical benefits of the activity of your choice, you will literally deconstruct the resistance network your brain builds and restore your confidence and motivation circuits.

Know it's not your fault

Teachers often blame themselves for students' problematic behavior, inability to "cover" each standard, and for not differentiating instruction to meet each student's needs. Know that you are not alone, but part of a growing majority of educators who question their abilities to continue teaching. You teach at a time when deep commitment and creativity is required to meet expectations. There is pressure to teach too much information and differentiate instruction to meet the needs of all students, but the necessary support resources are dwindling.

Feelings of burnout don't reflect your teaching skills. Teachers who question their ability to do their jobs correctly are often among those who hold themselves to the highest standards. They also make the best effort. When they are confronted with external forces - beyond their control - that limit their ability to achieve their goals, doubts, loss of confidence and burnout increase.

If you are exhausted, your brain is rewired into SURVIVAL MODE

What I offer from the nexus of my dual career as a neurologist and classroom teacher are interpretations and correlations from neuroscience research to teaching and learning. Neuroimaging studies reveal metabolic changes in brain regions where activity increases or decreases in response to emotional or sensory input.

There are specific and reproducible patterns of change in neural activity and brain structures associated with stress. In the high-stress state, the subject's scans reveal less activity in the higher, reflective brain and more activity in the lower, reactive brain that directs involuntary behaviors and emotional responses. Prolonged stress correlates with structural increases in the density and velocity of neuron-neuron connections in the emotion-driven reactive networks of the lower brain and corresponding decreases in connections in the conscious control centers of the prefrontal cortex.

The explanation for these changes is generally attributed to the brain's neuroplasticity of "neurons firing together, sticking together." The brain literally reconnects to be more efficient in conducting information through the circuits that are activated most frequently.

As you internalize your thwarted efforts to achieve your goals and interpret them as personal failure, your insecurity and stress activate and strengthen your brain's involuntary and reactive neural networks. As these circuits become automatic networks, the brain is less successful in problem solving and emotional control. When problems arise that previously would have been evaluated by higher brain reasoning, the dominant networks in the lower brain usurp control.

Restore your brain's default neural network!

The good news is that you can apply what you now understand about your brain's survival mode to voluntarily regain control of your choices. It is possible to activate the same neuroplasticity that gave dominance to the lower brain networks in the burnout state to build a new stronger default response. With more successful experiences reaching goals, you can restore the circuits that will direct your brain to access its highest cognitive resources for creative problem solving.

Since a repeated pattern of effort failure sets up the brain's survival response to hold back effort, you will need to reinforce the goal effort pattern that can lead to success. Your weapon for mass rebuilding may come from your brain's very powerful boost for its neurochemistry: dopamine and the pleasure it brings.

How to plan instructions using the video game template

The fuel that motivates the brain to persevere through increasing challenges, even through failed attempts, is dopamine. This neurochemical produces the pleasure of intrinsic satisfaction and increases motivation, curiosity, perseverance and memory. Dopamine is released when the brain makes a prediction or reaches a challenge and gets the feedback that it was correct. This can be in situations from the "Ah, I get it!" to understanding a joke, to the satisfaction of completing a marathon.

Just as the video game model can be applied to build a growth mindset in students, the same model can help you reconnect your mindset about your ability to achieve teaching goals in school. As in the video game model, to get the dopamine pleasure response from the challenges you have achieved, you will need to schedule frequent feedback recognition of incremental progress for your brain. You should set your "rewiring" goals based on their desirability and the suitability of the goals to be broken down into clear segments. This way, you can track the progress of your goals as you reach each gradual challenge. The pleasure of intrinsic motivation that will accompany the recognition of each progressive increment achieved in the goal path will keep your brain motivated to persevere.

Buy-in objective for the neuronal REWIRING of your brain

Buy-in and relevance are important in choosing your rewiring goal. Since your goal is to reconnect your brain's expectations that your efforts will produce progress, even though increasing challenge, you need to really want the goal. This is no time to challenge yourself with something you feel you need to do but are looking forward to doing, such as a diet, climbing stadium stairs, or flossing after every meal. Select a goal that you will enjoy along the way and at the finish line.

Goals are usually tangible. Some are visible, such as planting a garden or making pottery on a wheel. Others are auditory, like playing an instrument or physical, like learning Tai Chi. But your goal can also be the increased amount of time you do an activity such as journaling, yoga practice, or sketching.

Examples of "Rewiring" Goals

You'll find your buy-in goal, but here are some examples to give you an idea of how to structure your new goals.

Physical goals

Note that I didn't say exercise. It's not as motivating as "training" for a physical goal you want to achieve, even if they often overlap. If you want to run a 10K and if you like to run, the goal for an achievable challenge might be first of all building the distance starting with the base distance you run comfortably now. Then plot the increments that you will consider progressive hits, such as adding 0.5K per day or week. The increases will depend on what you consider both challenging and achievable. Once you hit 10K, speed can become the next goal, again plotted in incremental progress segments before starting.

Archery

Perhaps after watching The Hunger Games, archery has gained a new allure. Again, plan your achievable challenge increments step by step. Start with a home target (a low initial investment) and launch from a close but challenging range. As accuracy improves, move further back. Record your results, noting the distance of each improvement set as an achievable challenge.

Learning a language

But try this only if the buy-in is strong enough, such as definite plans to go to a country where the language is spoken.

Videography

If you like making high quality videos or PowerPoints using advanced computer software, try a hit right now, like the videos you can make on animoto.com.

Your rewired brain's default changes from Defeat to Power On

As you reach your incremental goals and have repeated dopamine reward experiences, you will literally change the circuitry in your brain. Repeated exertion/ reward experiences promote neuroplasticity and this creates a neural network that predicts positive outcomes in the new default network. This is because your "rewiring" goals have helped your brain build stronger and more connections in a memory model where effort brings pleasure. As with other unused networks, the previous lower brain stress activated active response network that you developed, the one that made you react to problems, will be eliminated from disuse.

Science Explains Women's Brains: This Is Why She Is Empathetic And "Multitasking"

The male and female brains are different from the moment of birth and it is they who guide impulses, values and the very vision of reality.

This difference is certainly the result of a chain of effects, which occurred over millennia, involving genetics, hormones, the brain, behaviors, and which do not imply any judgment of inferiority or superiority, of greater or lesser intelligence, but simply the recognition of the fact that during evolution, over the course of millennia, man and woman have had different roles and for this reason different brain adaptations have been made in the two sexes, capable of providing a neurobiological basis for behavioral differences.

Let's analyze the differences between the female and male brains.

A woman's brain weighs an average of 1,200 grams, a man's a little more: 1,350 grams. However, if the measurement is not absolute of the brain weight, but relative to the body weight, the difference vanishes and indeed there is a very slight one in favor of the female.

Over the past 100 years, women have outperformed men in intelligence, improving performance on IQ tests. And this is certainly not because their genes or brain size have changed, but because they have become more educated and have achieved greater possibilities of expression than in previous centuries.

In general, males have more neurons and women have more connections.

Connections. Scholars from the University of Pennsylvania have subjected 949 people, males and females of various ages, to an MRI, and found that in the male brain the connections run from front to back along the same hemisphere, while in the female the connections are also transversal, from the right hemisphere (linked to intuition) to the left one (linked to logical thinking).

This determines:

a) facilitated interhemispheric communication;

b) a more global mode of operation, more suitable for intuitive understanding of even complex problems than the rational and sequential procedure, more typical of the male sex.

We can say, in principle, that the man has a brain that follows patterns based more on rationality, while in the woman the cerebral functioning is more of an intuitive type, that in the man the functioning of the nervous circuits is more rigid while it is more plastic in women.

All this means that women are better at multitasking, that is, in doing more things together, they are more intuitive, they show greater empathy, they have better social skills. Males, on the other hand, excel in motor activities, where muscles are used, and are more capable of analyzing space, orienting themselves, understanding maps.

Number of neurons. While women have fewer neurons, they do have brain areas with at least 10% more neurons and connections. Harvard Medical School researchers, with the use of neuroimaging techniques (Rm; Pet; Spect; fRM), found a higher density of neurons in areas of the female temporal cortex connected with linguistic and emotional functions. This means that women are more likely to communicate emotions verbally and express feelings. Other more developed areas in the female brain are the hippocampus, the main center of emotion control and memory formation, and the set of circuits useful for observing the emotions of others. This is why, on average, as Louann Brizendine, a neuropsychiatrist who teaches at Berkley, writes, "women tend to develop unique and extraordinary skills: greater verbal agility, the ability to establish deep bonds of friendship, the almost mediumistic ability to decipher emotions and moods from facial expressions and tone of voice, and the mastery in placating conflicts. "

An important difference for the functional repercussions that can derive from it is that relating to an area considered the guardian of emotions, called amygdala due to the shape that makes it resemble an almond. The amygdala is the brain center of fear, anger, aggression, and is larger in men than in women.

But, beyond the size, the amygdala works differently in the two genders.

The female amygdala is more easily activated by emotional overtones. The stronger the amygdala response, the more details the hippocampus will record to store that experience in memory. Because women have a relatively larger hippocampus, they can remember the finest details of emotional experiences, their first dates, and the fiercest quarrels, while men barely remember that those events took place. In humans, however, the amygdala, which is the most primitive area of the brain, mainly maintains its most ancestral functions, those that register fears and trigger aggression. Consequently, it is easier for a man to get angry. This may explain why, faced with a situation of stress or anger or fear, the woman tends to activate mainly the emotional circuits, and the reaction always has an affective connotation; man activates the prefrontal cortex for which the response is predominantly motor and oriented to physical action. This is why many men can get into physical confrontation in seconds, while many women go to great lengths to avoid conflict. Even in these differences in behavior we can find an evolutionary explanation: in the face of a danger the woman had to protect the offspring, try to calm conflicts, while the man's task was to attack and drive away the aggressor. In their determination of the differences between the two brains, together with evolutionism, sex hormones also come into play. According to many scientists, the biological peculiarities of women - menstruation, pregnancy, breastfeeding, childbirth, childcare - strongly influence the cognitive, social and behavioral development of their brains.

We Have Two Brains

The revolutionary discovery of the abdominal brain: it remembers, it has neuroses and dominates the nobler "colleague". We only notice the brain in the head because it is the seat of consciousness, but - as they say - it is often the belly, or rather, the newly discovered nerve centers that decide.

The path of food from the stomach to the anus is long: first, 30 cm of duodenum, then 5 meters of small intestine, finally 1.5 m of large intestine. A second brain is needed to direct the 4 phases of peristalsis.

The brain (of the head) sends little information to the intestinal nervous system, which is largely independent. 90% of the information exchange is from the bottom up, from the abdomen to the brain.

Two very thin layers of a complex nervous system are hidden in the intestinal wall, the second largest after that of the head. These layers wrap around the digestive tract like a fishnet stocking. In this way they can coordinate the movements of the "peristaltic reflex" that moves food into the intestine.

The mechanism can be summarized as follows: the neurons in the intestinal wall sense where a bite of food (bolus) is, because they are stretched by the passing mass. Following this "perception", the "enterochromaffin" cells secrete serotonin, a protein that stimulates the nerve cells in the "submucosal plexus". These, in turn, send signals to the muscle cells which are activated, dilating and contracting the intestine.

If the peristaltic reflex is inhibited, for example due to low serotonin, constipation occurs, on the contrary an excessive stimulation due to too much serotonin causes diarrhea.

The abdominal brain is also responsible for passing information to the head. Some of these are obvious signs, such as vomiting in case of poisoning. But many other messages would be spontaneous, tied to the emotions, and imperceptible to the conscience: unconscious.

In all cultures, in idioms, in the common sense, the belly is traditionally the main seat (more than the brain) of feelings and emotions. But until now, for scientists, it was a simple tube governed by reflections; and for most citizens of the Western world only the most prosaic, slimy and noisy part of the human body.

Until someone thought to count the nerve fibers in the intestine. And it was discovered that the idioms were based on a scientific reality: in the belly there is a second brain, almost a copy of what we have in the head. It's not just for digestion. Like the brain in the head, the abdominal one also produces psychoactive substances that affect moods, such as serotonin, dopamine, but also opiate painkillers and even benzodiazepines, calming substances such as valium.

The colleague "below" also suffers from stress and neuroses

The abdominal brain, in short, works autonomously and sends more signals to the brain "in the head" than it receives from it. It helps to fix memories related to emotions. It can get sick, suffer from stress and develop its own neuroses. It can feel, think and remember. And it helps make decisions.

What was the need for two brains? "In the skull, everything did not fit" explains Michael Schemann, professor of physiology at the veterinary faculty in Hanover (Germany). "To pass the connections with the rest of the body, the neck would have to have a huge diameter. And then, just after birth, the newborn must eat, drink and digest: it is better for these fundamental functions to be autonomous".

During the formation of the embryo, therefore, a part of the nerve cells is incorporated in the head, another part goes into the abdomen: the connections between the two are held by the spinal cord and the vagus nerve. The second brain is entrusted with "visceral decisions", that is, spontaneous and unconscious: it therefore plays an important role in joy and pain.

A new science was born to study this second brain, neurogastroenterology. The foundations were laid in the mid-19th century by Leopold Auerbach, a German neurologist, who, observing the intestine under a microscope, noticed two very thin layers of nerve cells between two layers of muscle. And he discovered that this kind of fishnet stocking envelops the entire digestive tract, up to the rectum.

Same cells, same active ingredients and receptors: they are almost identical.

What are they for? Auerbach wondered. At that time, not much was known about the intestine except that it extracts energy from food. More than 30 tons of food and 50,000 liters of liquid pass through here in a lifetime. The heart, by comparison, is a primitive pump. Once chewed in the mouth and soaked with gastric juices in the stomach, the morsel, which has become chyme (i.e. mush), is compressed in the duodenum, the first part of the intestine 30 cm long. Here the secretions of the pancreas and gallbladder flow, the enzymes of which break down the chyme into very small molecules. Then the chyme passes into the small intestine, up to 5 meters long, where digestion takes place. Crushed food, fats, carbohydrates and proteins are absorbed into the blood and lymphatic vessels by billions of tiny villi that line the walls. After the small intestine, there is the large intestine, 1.5 meters long: it is used to reabsorb the 9 liters of liquids necessary for digestion. The molecular pumps of the large intestine absorb this water and return it to the body. At the end of the journey, food residues, dead cells and microorganisms are pushed towards the exit, the anus, thanks to a strong muscle bundle.

The network of nerve cells glimpsed by Auerbach is the management and control unit: it is not limited to analyzing the composition of food and coordinating the mechanisms of absorption and excretion. It also controls the speed of transit and other functions thanks to the balance between inhibitory and excitatory neurotransmitters, stimulating hormones and protective secretions.

What for us is just a steak, for the abdominal brain is a reality made up of millions of chemicals to be analyzed, to decide whether they are elements to be absorbed, a poison or a microorganism to be kept at a distance.

Because the brain of the abdomen is also the organizer of the front against the invaders. Its main task is to oversee the largest surface of the human body in contact with the outside.

It is the largest part in contact with the outside: we are hollow.

"Inside we are hollow," says Michael D. Gershon, a neuroscientist at Columbia University in New York, "the body comes into contact with the outside not only through the skin but also through the wall of the intestine. A tunnel so well built that it allows the surrounding environment to pass through us without doing us any damage".

In fact, about 500 species of potentially lethal beings live in the intestine. Even half of the stool is made up of dead bacteria. For this, the walls of the intestine must be the most efficient defense of the organism. This explains why 70% of the cells of the immune system are found there. And if poisons enter the abdomen, the abdominal brain warns the brain of the head which reacts with a predetermined strategy: vomiting, cramps and diarrhea.

If the poison is identified early it is eliminated from above, by the shortest route. If it is already halfway there, the peristaltic reflex comes into play. It is made up of wave contractions of the muscular wall of the intestine, which push the contents from the mouth towards the anus. These contractions are synchronized by the abdominal brain, stimulated by the pressure on its walls. It is enough for a mouthful of food to dilate a segment of the intestine, and the nerve cells begin to secrete neuromediators, i.e. proteins that are the chemical language of nerve cells, which inhibit or excite the muscle cells responsible for the reflex.

Typically, the further one enters the digestive system, the weaker the head brain's control becomes.

The mouth, parts of the esophagus and stomach still let themselves be told something from up there.

After the pylorus, the direction passes to the belly.

Gershon fell in love with the abdominal brain when he was a student, learning that serotonin, a neuromediator, affected moods and later discovering that 95% of serotonin is produced by the nerve cells of the gut and is also responsible for the peristaltic reflex.

When the belly gets sore it causes a lot of trouble.

Nobody took Gershon seriously until 1981, when the Australian Marcello Costa demonstrated that the nerve cells of the intestine produce serotonin, which in the meantime had turned out to be one of the many neuromediators of the nervous system. But it is not the only substance secreted by the abdominal brain, which is a huge chemical factory because it produces about forty neuromediators with which it communicates through the brain of the head.

In fact, the cells of both brains speak the same chemical language. And this explains why Alzheimer's and Parkinson's patients often find the same type of lesions in both brains. And because psychiatric drugs also act on the intestine and gastrointestinal drugs also on the brain. A gastric hormone, serotonin, is being tested in the treatment of autism, a psychiatric disease. An anti-migraine sedates the overactive intestines. Pain relievers calm certain inflammations of the digestive tract. And some antidepressants act on the brain mood, but also on the abdominal brain causing diarrhea or constipation.

The latest experimental therapy for irritable bowel is the result of studies on the abdominal brain. 20% of the population suffers from irritable colon: it causes pain in the abdomen, irregular bowel movements, accumulation of air in the intestine. It is not known why the colon of these patients is malfunctioning. The culprit, according to Schemann, is the abdominal brain.

Gershon argues that the abdominal brain is prone to neurosis. The communication between the two brains is however dominated by the one in the belly. This is where 90% of the messages go straight to the head. Most of these messages are unconscious, that is, they happen without us becoming aware of them. We perceive them only when they are warning signs that trigger reactions of malaise.

Depressed people feel all the movements of their intestines

Emeran Mayer, a professor at the University of California, found that some of the messages from the abdominal brain arrive in the limbic system, located in the center of the brain of the head. This area has the task of processing negative signals and suppressing unpleasant sensations. "It's a bit like the phenomenon of the pinching sweater" explains Mayer "after a while you don't feel it anymore".

The stimuli coming from the intestine are perceived only if they exceed a rather high threshold, while those suffering from irritable bowel, according to Mayer, would have a lower threshold and would feel every bowel movement. "Depressed and anxious people also have similar sensations," Mayer says.

Why is the threshold lowered? Maybe because of the stress.

If the brain perceives the head tension and fear, mustering intestine cells that produce irritants such as histamine. This protein in turn activates the nerve cells of the digestive tract which cause the muscle cells to contract – causing cramping or diarrhea.

The alarm signal then goes to the brain of the head which retransmits it downwards and so on. If the anxiety does not subside, the circle closes and the symptoms become chronic.

The stresses of the past also remain etched in the belly

The abdominal brain would even be equipped with memory that uses the same molecules as the brain of the head to fix memories: the stresses of the past are thus imprinted in the brain and abdomen, says Schemann, making the brain-abdomen axis hypersensitive throughout the life. And this explains why children who suffer from colic in childhood generally have a higher risk of becoming adults with irritable bowel disease.

Mice exposed as infants to stressful situations are also hypersensitive adults, with intestinal symptoms similar to those of irritable bowel.

And 40 percent of irritable bowel patients typically also suffer from anxiety and depression.

What melancholy and fear then arise in the intestine?

"Our results show that, just as hunger and satiety affect mood, the origin of other moods can be hidden in the abdominal brain , including classic depression," says Mayer. However, this research is still in its infancy.

Whenever the intestine contracts and emits serotonin or other neuromediators, the information travels along the vagus fimo nerve to the brain of the head. Where they are translated into malaise or cheerfulness, fatigue or vitality, good or bad mood.

The belly also dreams during the REM sleep phase

"We can even say that the abdominal brain thinks," says Schemann. "It is functionally organized, works with a series of circuits, is able to register different states and react autonomously: in short, it has everything an integrative nervous system needs".

What is certain is that the abdomen creates the atmosphere for the head. The head is the "bank of emotions" that collects all the reactions and data, especially in the anterior cortex, behind the forehead, particularly linked to the abdomen.

In short, the brain of the abdomen tells its version to the brain of the head, creates its "emotional profile" and prepares a "bed of sensations", even for the night. And in fact, during the rem phase of sleep, when it produces sweet waves and is filled with dreams, even the bowels begin to sway thanks to the serotonin. "And don't you have bad dreams after a heavy meal?" Mayer wonders.

With these waves the brain of the head fixes the memories with their load of emotions.

The more fixed the emotions are, the better the decisions will be next time.

"In the next few years we may discover that the brain of the abdomen is the biological matrix of the unconscious. A discovery as important to humans as Copernicus' discovery of the solar system," says Gershon.

The Dialogue Between Emotion and Reason

"Reason and passion are the rudder and sail of our sailing soul"

Khalil Gibran

Often people tell of having done something that they only realized later, and which maybe they even regretted bitterly. American writer Ambrose Gwinnett Bierce could not have expressed this concept better: "Speak without controlling your anger and you will have the best speech you will ever regret." To this there is a neuroscientific explanation that defines how the mental processing of stimuli works, and therefore the emotional, cognitive and behavioral reaction.

Joseph E. LeDoux, American neuroscientist, director of the "Center for the Neuroscience of Fear and Anxiety" in New York, is a scholar among the greatest experts on emotions, since his major research has been concerned with the functioning of the limbic system in to the emotions and ways in which the human personality is expressed. LeDoux has discovered some brain mechanisms that have made it possible to better understand how the cognitive and emotional processing of signals entering the brain works.

Until LeDoux's contribution, previous neuroscientists, albeit in their specific theories, had always described the development of emotions in the brain according to this process.

Here's how this process goes:

Sensory receptors pick up the emotional stimulus, transform it into an electrical signal and send it to the thalamus.

The thalamus sends the electrical signal to the neocortex.

The neocortex integrates the information and elaborates the perception of the stimulus, then sends the response to the limbic system.

The limbic system processes an emotional response and sends it to the body to implement it.

And here is also a brief description of the components of this process:

Sensory receptors are specialized cells responsible for receiving external and internal stimuli in the body and for transmitting them, translated into electrical impulses, through the afferent nerve fibers to the central nervous system.

The thalamus is an area belonging to the diencephalon, the innermost part of the brain, specialized in processing stimuli that come from inside the body. The thalamus has the function of transmitting electrical impulses from sensory receptors to the cerebral cortex.

The neocortex is the part of the cerebral cortex that has phylogenetically developed most recently, and represents about 90% of the human brain surface. It is the seat of higher cognitive functions: learning, memory and language; that is, those functions of more recent genetic development in the course of human evolution.

The limbic system represents a set of brain formations, belonging to the telencephalon and diencephalon, which perform the task of controlling emotions and behavioral reactions related to survival.

LeDoux, with his studies, discovered that the neural pathway of emotions already identified by other neuroscientists was not the only one. In fact, he highlighted that the amygdala, a part of the limbic system that manages emotions, and especially fear, unlike what was previously thought, actually covers a more privileged position in the brain, and if necessary, it has the power to checkmate the neocortex and to take control of the mind (LeDoux JE, 1993).

Le Doux discovered that there are two neural pathways that process emotional stimuli (LeDoux JE, 1994):

A high neural pathway that passes through the neocortex and then reaches the amygdala.

A low neural pathway that bypasses the neocortex and directly reaches the amygdala.

The high neural pathway processes an emotional response through the neocortex.

The low neural pathway is activated parallel to the high one, and bypassing the neocortex, like a shortcut, through a thin bundle of nerve fibers, directly connects the thalamus to the amygdala.

What is the difference between the two neural pathways?

The high neural pathway is slower but gains in completeness. In fact, involving more brain areas it takes about double the time to process the stimuli, but on the other hand it provides a much more detailed and comprehensive response.

The low neural pathway, on the other hand, is incomplete but gains in speed. After all, not passing through the neocortex takes less time. The price that this path pays is that it obtains a partial recording of the elements of the experience, only those with a high emotional impact captured by the amygdala. So, if on the one hand it is a very fast way, on the other it elaborates a partial and incomplete knowledge of the events (Goleman D., 1996).

The high neural pathway represents the neural mechanism of normal situations, where by normal we mean the usual and regular life situations, those in which you may have the time to pause to reflect before elaborating a mental response. For example, when you are carefully choosing a dress to buy, or when you are organizing what to do for the day, listening to emotional predispositions in some ways and rational ones in others. In these, as in other similar situations, while the amygdala prepares its emotional action plan, based on an approximate knowledge of the experience, the neocortex in parallel records more accurately the details, and taking into account all information, including that sent from the amygdala, it selects the emotional response it deems best suited to that experience. And the choice that the neocortex makes is based on the evaluation of probable gains but also of losses, or on the relationship between risks and benefits (Davidson R. J, Jackson DC, Kalin NH, 2000)

The low neural pathway, on the other hand, represents the neural mechanism of alarm situations, when you are faced with dangerous events and time is precious, and you have to quickly decide whether to flee or attack to best guarantee survival. It is a circuit designed to deal with emergencies and ensure survival. This is why, when the amygdala is reached by an alarming emotional stimulus, it is activated to the point of even being able to checkmate the neocortex, completely defusing its functions, and taking command of the whole brain. In doing so, the amygdala concentrates all psychic energies solely and exclusively on surviving. The amygdala, therefore, is able both to process the emotional response autonomously, and to send it to the various parts of the body to transform it into real action. And precisely on the basis of this mechanism it happens that in an emergency situation, such as fleeing from a burning house or getting to safety from a storm, a detailed memory of the experience is not kept, only certain details are remembered. After all, the amygdala, having recognized the danger and taken the lead, in making a decision on what to do is based on those few dangerous stimuli that it has registered and processed, and does not fully memorize the experience, as the neocortex would do (LeDoux EJ, 1994). This circuit is satisfied with partial and incomplete information because as LeDoux explains: "You don't need to know exactly what it is, to know that it can be dangerous". (Goleman D., 1996)

It's nice to see how nature has thought of everything, and has endowed us with two mechanisms, one just in case.

What's the problem?

The problem is that sometimes these mechanisms, like so many other mechanisms of nature, get jammed and confused. And they do it especially when there is no dialogue between the amygdala and the neocortex, between emotions and reasons.

In fact, it may happen that the lower neural pathway takes over in situations that only apparently seem like an emergency, but which in reality are not, and then problems can occur. After all, relying on little information in situations that would require more careful consideration can be a problem.

Let's imagine, for example, that we are faced with a dog coming in our direction, and imagine that the amygdala, associating this situation with a similar one from many years ago, when a dog ran after us and we were scared to death, put us on the alert and pushed us to flee madly in the midst of city traffic; when in reality that dog is going its own way, regardless of our presence. Let us reflect on how much our behavior, in this case, rather than guaranteeing our survival, as was in the good intentions of the amygdala, actually made us take a great risk. And why? Because the amygdala records information according to an associative method: it compares present experiences with past ones, and it is enough for it to find an element in common to identify two different situations. It is an approximate and outdated method (Goleman D., 1996), it is based on little information and uses action plans from the past. All this, if it can be useful in real emergency situations, where a detail is enough to understand that you are in danger, and where it is sufficient to repeat behavioral patterns of the past to guarantee survival, it is not useful in other situations. In this example, in fact, the amygdala was fired in a situation where it shouldn't have been fired, and the little information on which it was based made it wrong, it made 2 + 2 = 7.

However, it may happen that even the high neural pathway takes over in situations that only apparently would seem to be analyzed in detail. And even in this case, with the intervention of the neocortex alone, there is a risk of engaging in behavior that is not suitable and inappropriate to the situation (Goleman D., 1996).

Let's imagine, for example, that a friend of ours is telling a joke and we are there listening to him, and imagine that we, instead of laughing and concentrating on the ironic aspect of the story, were going to analyze the details, telling our friend that the joke proposes a scenario that is not real and that the story does not make logical sense. Well, it is clear that, by concentrating on the analysis of the facts, we would lose the very meaning of the joke and the emotion that goes with it. And also, in this case, the massive intervention of the logical analysis carried out by the neocortex puts the amygdala in checkmate, which, not being able to make its emotional contribution, deprives the experience of its cheerfulness. The result of all this is that the neocortex has recorded too many details, and this, if on other occasions it would have been of great help, in this case instead it was totally out of place and completely misplaced, losing that healthy laughter that joke wanted to arouse. The neocortex, despite all the data collected, did the math badly, it made 2 + 2 = 0.

What is the solution?

Clearly the solution lies in trying to integrate and harmonize emotion and reason as much as possible, in such a way that each resource can inform and enrich the other, since each without the other would fall into error.

And luckily nature has thought of everything, and has equipped us with a "knob" built into our brain that allows us to manage and calm the strong emotional waves. This knob is located in the neocortex, and more precisely in the prefrontal lobes. The prefrontal lobes regulate our behavior, our actions and even our emotional reactions (Davidson R. J, Jackson DC, Kalin NH, 2000). They are the center of executive functions, that is, the mind's ability to plan and organize action plans for a goal, including emotional goals. It then happens that while the amygdala is alarmed to trigger an anxious and impulsive emotional reaction, the prefrontal lobes modulate these reactions and make them more analytical and appropriate to the situations. And the same is true of the excessive activation of the logical-analytical faculties of the neocortex. Here, too, the connection between the prefrontal lobes and the amygdala integrate emotions with the reasons for planning a behavior that is as balanced and appropriate to the situation as possible.

The solution is therefore in dialogue, in harmony and in the integration of emotion and reason. Which often occurs spontaneously, but just as often it could fail. Especially when faced with situations with a strong emotional impact. The remedy can be in the supervision of one's brain, since, despite being a wonderful device, it does not always manage to give its best on its own, it needs our help.

Daniel J. Siegel, a psychiatrist who heads the Mindsight Institute at the University of California at Los Angeles, is a famous neuroscientist who was among the first to recognize the ability to mindsight (seeing the mind) as a tool for psychological well-being. According to Siegel, it is essential to monitor mental activity and actively encourage it to be integrated, harmonious and balanced. A passive attitude could lead to being overwhelmed and crushed by incorrect mental activity of the brain (Siegel DJ, Amadei G. Prunas A., 2010). After all, life is not that simple, and the abilities of the brain can be compromised by the events and experiences of life. That is why it is vital to make the effort to observe your own mind and become aware of how it is working. Only in this way can we intervene to make corrections.

It is important to remember to monitor your mind, only in this way can you become aware of what you are doing, and only in this way can you intervene if you are "making a mountain out of a molehill". Self-awareness is the ability to be aware of what is happening within oneself, and it is the key that opens the doors of well-being, allowing us to know what our reason is doing and what our emotions are doing, and eventually, it allows us to improve their work.

Are We Sure That Thinking of The Mind as Something "Inside" Us Is Useful?

What is the use of knowing brain processes: to improve, manage emotions better or be able to communicate effectively?

Is our essence really something within us?

In this chapter we will look at the real risks of thinking that this essence is our brain or our personality. My proposal (which here simplifies a pragmatic and interactionist approach) is that it is better to think of the mind as something outside. It is better to think that you are outside. Yes: outside like balconies.

The theory you have about yourself: what do you need it for?

Let's start with the things we need. If you want to communicate better or manage your emotions or believe more in yourself and you want to "do it seriously", you have to assume that you work or modify something that you perceive constant: here I call it "mind", but if you want, we can call it "character", "Personality", "I", "self-awareness", "identity", etc.

If there were not this something constant, there would be no need to "change" or "improve": it would be enough to want to do something to do it (or learn how to do it). No obstacles, no demotivation, no laziness: you tell yourself "don't be embarrassed" and stop being so; "Start and keep a diet" and you do it; "Be more sociable" and you are.

It would be nice, but we know that this is not the case: there is something constant that on the one hand binds us to our unwanted habits and on the one hand allows us to have other good and useful habits.

It is what, if generally called mind, is subjectively experienced as me or me (and it is no coincidence that my improvement course is called Me-Lab).

If you want to "improve" on something, you have to work on this something constantly, or rather: even if you are not aware of it, you will use tools and techniques built on some theory of the mind.

One of the greatest psychologists of the last century, Kurt Lewin, is remembered for this sentence

" There is nothing more practical than a good theory "

This is because the theory we use (sometimes completely unconsciously) makes us see, think and act in a certain way and not in many other possible ways. A theory is a very practical tool, as a flathead screwdriver is very useful, but only with a certain type of screws and with a certain type of purposes.

But a scientist struggling with books and university laboratories does not say this, in fact, even if it is rarely reported, the quote is not from Lewin, but it is a phrase that the psychologist reports and attributes to an entrepreneur, that is to a person strongly interested in outcomes of their business.

Let's get back to us, it becomes necessary to understand if, while you speak and use some tools, the theory of mind that you are unknowingly adopting will be useful to you or not.

Is the answer within you?

We always remain on the usefulness: when we think "I have potentialities inside me that I can't get out", what theory of mind do we use?

Let's try to think about the risks in telling it like this.

For this theory you are more inside than what you show outside, the "real you" is inside you.

How do you find it? Is there a probe?

You will tell me: no, I use introspection.

Well: what do you inspect? Do you lock yourself in meditation somewhere and what are you looking for? What are you doing? What questions do you ask yourself?

Do you think that you will find serenity or self-esteem within yourself?

How will they emerge or reveal themselves?

Do you think you will hear a voice that will at some point solemnly describe who you are, how you will have to behave and what you will have to do in your life?

And do you think that then you, so internally enlightened, will be able to travel around the world, go to work, relate to others with greater capacity and awareness?

If so, pay attention: it is a widespread theory, very fascinating, but useful only in specific areas and at specific times.

There are not many of the things you learned in this theory:

- to walk you have not meditated months in the lotus position and then rise with momentum, elegantly moving feet and legs with the torso erect and a proud look. Not even to speak. Not even for maths or driving a car or writing a poem or playing football.

You have acquired nothing of what is human in the solitude of introspection.

If anything, introspection, reflection, contemplation and other practices may have served you to organize thoughts, to calm emotions, have greater clarity and serenity of mind, but (except for connections with the divine) all to then direct you towards something that was not inside you, but outside of you: you understood that it was better to leave your job, you felt your feelings for a person in a deeper way, you decided to go on a journey or you just got a better mood functional to the resumption of daily life.

You did not find your true self: when it went well, you found a way to do something that represented you in the way you were able to do it. If, after meditating, you decide to climb a mountain or build a company, introspection will have swept away the doubts, but it will not have provided you with the tools to make your choice: that "yourself" (who climbs the mountain or creates activity) you will find it while you are implementing the decision made.

In summary: this is a theory that helps you remove and clarify and then act. If you use it to "find" yourself or a definitive answer to your "why", you will continue to wander into the void of dissatisfaction.

Does the brain command?

The better neuropsychologists (and from there down to the gurus of social networks) explain to us that our emotions depend on the amygdala [For the uninitiated, the amygdala is a small structure placed at the center of each cerebral hemisphere (therefore each has two of us)].

If you take a course on fear management, someone will come up with the amygdala sooner or later, but not in the literal sense, also because they wouldn't know what to do with it. And it seems obvious to me that no one would know what to do with an amygdala in their hands.

However, in that course on emotions, they will show you colored drawings with arrows to make you understand how your fear works.

What theory of mind are they using?

Rhetorical question: a "neurological" theory: your mind is the sum of brain processes and the fear process involves the amygdala.

But what is the use of hearing you explain the neurophysiological mechanisms related to an emotion?

Two things:

The first has a rhetorical function (didactic or marketing): as research at Yale has shown, peppering a psychological explanation with neurological references leads people to consider it more "scientific" and, therefore, "true". This favor thinking that the trainer is an "expert" you can trust and, therefore, better apply the contents of his course or buy his products or services.

The second, to find a solution consistent with that theory.

The problem is that your trainer talks to you about the amygdala only because he has read a few books in no particular order, without inserting it into a theory of mind and, above all, without thinking about whether that theory is usable by you.

Because, let's remember, if we had our two amygdalae in our hands, we wouldn't know what to do with them.

To accurately influence the functioning of the amygdala we need a tool that acts directly on the brain structure. Usually a scalpel or electrode or drug.

Do you find these useful for dealing with fear?

If so, well: get up immediately from that training course and contact a neurosurgeon or a neuropsychiatrist, because they are the experts in that theory and those tools.

If you believe that it is possible to influence the functioning of your amygdala through thoughts, words and actions, you must know that no research scientifically demonstrates how this can happen.

This is easy to understand.

We can measure the electrical activity and change in blood flow of a brain area, but we don't have a tool to scientifically define what an emotion is outside of a psychological theory. Neurology deals with gray matter, psychology with theories that define what we are talking about.

Because, and this will surprise you, not for all psychologists is the fear of a rat or getting a shock inside a metal cage is comparable to the fear of a parent waiting for the return of his teenage daughter on Saturday night or the fear of a football player to take a penalty kick, or the fear of dying of an elderly person or that of being left by a beloved. Although it may seem strange, for many of us, these are different fears and, moreover, neuroimaging tells us that they involve almost the entire brain in a different way ...

Your neurosurgeon should work hard on it.

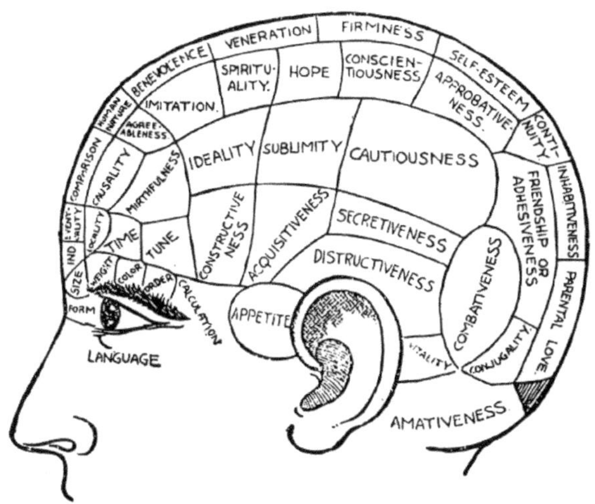

In summary, this theory is only useful to experts in the field to conduct research, deepen differential diagnoses and broaden the knowledge of neuropsychology which, perhaps unfortunately, is still a long way off from helping people using physical tools, but can offer psychological tools in reference to small scraps of the human mind directly related to neurological phenomena.

So: if you believe that everything depends on the brain, you are implicitly saying that you have no operational tool to modify its functioning. Unless you consider psychological tools which, however, if they were to be consistent with your theory, should concern such limited fields of your experience that alone they would be of no use. And so you will have to use broader psychological tools, but you will be doing it in bulk because you will be using tools that were not born from the theory you have adopted up to that point.

It's a mess! Are we outside like balconies?

A tool must be used in the proper context. I can't use a screwdriver to tighten a bolt. Maybe I can use it to drive a nail, but I would certainly be more successful if I used a hammer for the nails and the screwdriver for the screws.

If your purpose is to change your behavior or your emotions in some contexts, it is best that you adopt tools created specifically for those contexts.

Thinking of the mind as something inside you won't help you. Better to think of your mind as something outside of yourself.

Better to think that your mind is the sum of your actions, emotions and feelings in time and space. You'd better geolocate it.

To deal with the idea of yourself while on retreat inside a cave is to fantasize about practical little useful generalizations. Dealing with yourself when you're starting your day tomorrow morning at 7:12 is having the opportunity to feel and try to change something.

Thinking that a specific area of the brain is affecting your life is an idea that should immediately lead you to a visit to a neurologist.

Thinking that the way you spoke to your co-workers yesterday afternoon was not effective, however, will direct you to analyze the situation and take steps for next week's meeting.

Believing that you lack self-esteem will put you in anticipation that someone or something will fill that void (perhaps by pouring a few liters of self-esteem inside you).

Summary and usefulness

Still paraphrasing Kurt Lewin, do you want to know yourself? Then try to change! You learn by doing and, therefore, you will learn more about yourself by experimenting. Use the moments of reflection to understand what worked in reality and what didn't, but then take action.

The brain is necessary, but it is also very complicated. Let's leave it to the experts. If neuroscience fascinates you, also have the humility to see how you are not able to apply it to your concrete life: read and study as you would for astronomy, a wonderful subject that is helpful to humanity if handled by expert astronomers, but which you will only rarely know how to apply to your daily life.

Mind is nothing concrete: it is a definition. Think of it as if it were outside of you, in the world and amongst people, and try to change it one interaction at a time.

<u>Anger in children: amygdala and surroundings, what happens?</u>

It is well known that in managing anger our children, to varying degrees and with due environmental and temperamental considerations, have to deal with the growth of neurological functions and the maturation of emotional capacities.

A nice summary.

WHAT HAPPENS IN THE BRAIN AND BODY OF A CHILD IN ANGER?

Our brain consists of two basic parts: the upper brain (cortex) and the lower brain (sub-cortex). With other mammals we share the structure of the lower brain which is the seat of the circuits of all the most primitive and instinctual emotions.

The circuit of anger is also there and all of us, without exception, have one. One of the most important anatomical structures in the anger circuit is the amygdala, which is activated when we perceive a threat to our physical or psychological integrity around us.

Of course, it is important that the amygdala is very fast at registering threats and because of this it can sometimes be a bit gross. For example, imagine you are walking in a forest. At a certain point you see a black shape on the path that seems to point towards you: your amygdala will immediately trigger the alarm in the brain and in the body, because at first sight it could be a danger, for example a poisonous snake. Our body therefore prepares for a defense reaction, either to flee (fear) or to attack (anger).

It only takes a few seconds, however, for you to realize that in reality that shape is just a broken branch and so the alarm goes off. Who is it that tells the amygdala that it was a false alarm?

It is the higher brain that has this task and that, through reflective thinking, "calms" the body and the brain by telling them: "Don't worry, it's just a branch". However, if it had really been a snake it would have been essential to react quickly and there would have been no time to ponder the various options. Our amygdala therefore has the fundamental task of always being alert to anything that could threaten our safety, both physical and psychological, but the upper brain has the task of moderating and calming the reactions triggered by the amygdala, and it does release calming substances, such as gamma-amino-butyric acid (GABA), which is a real "natural" anxiolytic.

The ability to "moderate" one's emotional reactions based on an assessment of the context and circumstances is not something innate, like anger, but it must be learned.

Preschoolers are unable to do this on their own, but are completely dependent on adults who, with loving interactions, "lend" their minds and words to them to help lower stimulation levels.

When the stress level of a relationship is very high, i.e. when the relationship is based on corporal and psychological punishment, insults, humiliations, emotional coldness, neglect, screams, refusal to comfort, etc., and the child is only faced with this circumstance, stress substances enter the circulation and serotonin levels decrease.

Serotonin, a substance produced by the brain, is used to lower the levels of aggression and impulsiveness, and when its levels drop, children become more inclined to vent their anger in actions.

However, if an adult is able to act as an "emotional regulator" for the child, it will help him develop a well-established system of stress relief in his brain, so that the child learns that emotions, and anger in particular, can also be thought and communicated, as well as acted out.

When a child is invaded by anger, however, he reaches a state of over-arousal that inhibits any kind of reflection about his own behavior and the consequences it may have on others.

The child in anger is unable to put himself in the other's shoes and, when the brain circuit of anger is activated, attacking the other may seem like the only possible solution. In this sense, a child trapped in his own anger has very few alternatives. The sense of peace and calm satisfaction are instead induced by two particular types of substances that are released in his brain: oxytocin and opiates.

These substances are produced in a child's brain, especially as a result of affectionate interactions (kisses, hugs, cuddles, kind and affectionate verbal exchanges, engaging games, smiles, caresses, etc.) with attachment figures and other significant figures. If every time a child experiences stress and discomfort there is an adult who is constantly ready to comfort him, understand him, offer him behavioral alternatives, he will slowly develop that same self-calming ability that will allow him, later on, to reassure himself when he finds himself in similar situations, thus having a real alternative to simply discharging his anger and discontent.

Conversely, if a child in childhood has experienced constant or intermittent loneliness or punishment when he has found himself in situations of discomfort, he will not be able to independently develop the ability to "calm" the lower brain, literally remaining a prisoner of a sole possibility: to act on one's anger. I hope that from what has been said so far it is clear how punitive or angry interventions by a parent or an educator in front of a child's outbursts not only serve no purpose, but risk increasing the level of threat perceived by the small child, who can feel attacked, thus increasing his already high level of stress.

Brain Hemispheres – What Are They? Anatomy and Functions

In General

The cerebral hemispheres are the two hemispherical portions of nervous tissue, inside the skull, which actually make up the human brain.

Also, thanks to the presence of a deep groove between them, the two cerebral hemispheres are distinguished as right cerebral hemisphere and left cerebral hemisphere; the cerebral hemispheres are only apparently symmetrical: under the microscopic and functional profile, in fact, they are extremely different.

Each cerebral hemisphere has an outer layer of gray matter, called the cerebral cortex (or neocortex), and a deeper component, including both white matter and gray matter, generically called the subcortical component.

Through the cerebral cortex and the subcortical component, the cerebral hemispheres control fundamental mental-cognitive functions, such as voluntary movements, sensory abilities, language, memory, learning, etc.

Definition of Cerebral Hemispheres

Looking at any reproduction of the human brain, the cerebral hemispheres immediately jump to the eye: they are those two hemispheres characterized by grooves, ridges and lobules, and separated by a deep groove, which occupy a large part of the skull.

Curiosity

The presence of the cerebral hemispheres can be found in the brain of all vertebrates.

Brain: a brief review

The brain, or telencephalon or brain proper, is the most voluminous and most specialized portion of that large and complex nervous structure, which is called the brain.

A vital organ, the brain takes its place in the skull, above other brain components equally important for life, such as the diencephalon, the brainstem and the cerebellum.

Anatomy

Protected by the skull, the cerebral hemispheres are arranged in such a way that one belongs to the right half of the human body and the other to the left half; as a logical consequence of this arrangement, the cerebral hemisphere located on the right is called the right cerebral hemisphere, while the cerebral hemisphere located on the left is called the left cerebral hemisphere.

As will be seen later, the distinction of the cerebral hemispheres into the right and left is important not only from the anatomical point of view, but also from the functional point of view.

The cerebral hemispheres develop antero-posterior (or ventro-dorsal), with the base oriented downwards and the curvature upwards.

As anticipated, to divide the right cerebral hemisphere from the left cerebral hemisphere there is a deep and evident groove: arranged in such a way as to run through the brain in an antero-posterior direction, this groove is the so-called median longitudinal fissure (NB: the term longitudinal is a reminder of its antero-posterior course).

The median longitudinal fissure is also known because an important reflection fold of the dura mater, called the cerebral sickle, descends along it.

Each cerebral hemisphere has an outer layer of gray matter (neurons devoid of myelin), called the cerebral cortex (or neocortex), and an inner, deeper component, including both white matter (neurons wrapped in a layer of myelin) and of gray matter, generically called subcortical component.

If it is true that the cerebral hemispheres are separated by the median longitudinal fissure, it is equally true that there are, at their base, some junction structures, also important for the exchange of information, which take the generic name of interhemispheric commissures.

Macroscopic Anatomy

Macroscopically, the cerebral hemispheres appear as a mirror image of each other; however, upon closer inspection, at least two subtle differences emerge: the greater size of the right cerebral hemisphere compared to the left and the slightly more advanced position of the right cerebral hemisphere compared to the left.

Poles of the Cerebral Hemispheres

To facilitate the macroscopic description of the cerebral hemispheres, anatomists identify on each of the two 3 poles: the frontal pole, anteriorly, the occipital pole, posteriorly, and the temporal pole, on both sides.

Microscopic Anatomy

From the point of view of cytoarchitecture (in other words, at the microscopic level), the two cerebral hemispheres show evident asymmetry from each other (i.e. they are different), especially at the level of the cerebral cortex: the differences concern the functions of the constituent neurons, the types of receptors and the quantities of neurotransmitters.

Cerebral cortex

Extremely important from the functional point of view, the cerebral cortex is, in both cerebral hemispheres, a layer of gray matter about 2.5 millimeters thick.

The cerebral cortex comprises over 20 million neurons and more than 300 trillion nerve synapses; such high numbers, despite a limited thickness, are possible thanks to the particular architecture of the cerebral cortex itself: the latter, in fact, presents an alternation of grooves and ridges (better known as convolutions), which it significantly increases its extension (some studies speak of an extension equal to about 2,000 square centimeters).

The cerebral cortex of each hemisphere of the brain is ideally divided into 4 major areas, called the frontal lobe, temporal lobe, parietal lobe and occipital lobe.

Did you know that ...

The cerebral cortex is present only in the mammalian brain.

The cerebral cortex characterized by furrows and convolutions is typical of the most evolved mammals (including humans).

Subcortical component

The subcortical component of the cerebral hemispheres includes:

Clusters of white matter, on which the cerebral cortex rests;

Formations of gray matter (which should not be confused with the cerebral cortex), surrounded by the aforementioned white matter;

The lateral cerebral ventricles.

Subcortical White Substance

Known as a whole as a semi-oval center (because of its shape), the subcortical white matter is organized, in its deepest part, in thick bands called capsules; interposed above all between the nuclei of the base, the white matter capsules present in the cerebral hemispheres are divided into 3 types: the internal capsules, the external capsules and the extreme capsules.

Subcortical Gray Matter

The gray matter formations present in each of the two cerebral hemispheres are:

Amygdala.

Hippocampus. Morphologically similar to a seahorse, the hippocampus is involved in various processes, including: the consolidation of information from short and long-term memory, the processing of spatial maps and spatial memory.

Nuclei of the base. Closely connected to the cerebral cortex, the thalamus and the brainstem, the nuclei of the base are divided into various components, which take the name of: dorsal striatum (nucleus caudate and putamen), ventral striatum (nucleus accumbent and olfactory tubercle), pale globe, pale ventral, substantia nigra and subthalamic nucleus.

The nuclei of the base are associated with various functions, including: control of voluntary movements, eye movement, procedural learning, learning habits; furthermore, they also appear to be involved in emotion, decision making and motivational states.

Olfactory bulb. Located inferior to the frontal lobe, the olfactory bulb plays a pivotal role in the process of perception of odors (olfaction).

It should be noted that the olfactory bulb communicates with other structures and regions of the brain, including the amygdala, the hippocampus, the substantia nigra and the orbitofrontal cortex (region of the prefrontal cortex of the frontal lobe) and the hippocampus.

Curiosity

Amygdala, hippocampus and the nucleus accumbens (nucleus of the base) are three elements of the so-called limbic system.

The limbic system is a complex of brain structures with a key role in emotional reactions, behavioral responses, memory processes and smell.

Lateral Cerebral Ventricles

There are two lateral cerebral ventricles, or simply lateral ventricles, one for each cerebral hemisphere. Comparable to a Y lying on the left flank, the lateral ventricles border all four cerebral lobes. It should be remembered that, together with the other cerebral ventricles (third and fourth ventricles), the lateral ventricles provide for the production of the cerebrospinal fluid and its distribution in the central nervous system.

Interhemispheric commissures

The interhemispheric commissures present in the human brain are: the corpus callosum, the commissure of the fornix and the anterior commissure. The corpus callosum is placed between the two cerebral hemispheres and, in addition to physically uniting them, allows for an exchange of information between them.

The commissure of the fornix connects the hippocampus of the right hemisphere with the hippocampus of the left hemisphere.

Finally, the anterior commissure is responsible for creating communication between the two temporal lobes.

Did you know that ...

The corpus callosum is present only in placental mammals (or Euteri).

Where are the Cerebral Hemispheres: Boundaries and Relationships?

As parts of the brain, the cerebral hemispheres are located inside the skull, protected by the frontal bone, above-anteriorly, by the two temporal bones, laterally, the two parietal bones, above, and by the occipital bone, posteriorly.

The cerebral hemispheres constitute the apex of the brain and encephalon. Under the corpus callosum (therefore inferior to the main interhemispheric commissure), the diencephalon develops and, immediately below the diencephalon, there is the midbrain (first portion of the brain stem).

The lower border of the anterior section of the cerebral hemispheres borders on the orbital cavities, while the lower border of the posterior section borders on the cerebellum.

Development

From which embryonic structure do the Cerebral Hemispheres originate? Regarding their embryonic origin, the cerebral hemispheres derive, together with the other parts of the brain, from a prenatal nervous structure called the forebrain. In vertebrates, the forebrain is one of the three primitive cerebral vesicles, from which the entire nervous system derives (the other two are the midbrain and hindbrain).

In humans, the forebrain is the prenatal nervous structure from which the diencephalon also originates.

Fetal Development of the Cerebral Hemispheres: when do they appear?

The forebrain differs into brain and diencephalon around the 5th week of pregnancy (3rd week from conception); the cerebral hemispheres, however, begin to form between the 7th and 8th week of pregnancy (5th-6th week from conception). The formation of the cerebral hemispheres includes the generation of the cerebral cortex, amygdala, hippocampus, basal ganglia, and lateral ventricles.

Function

Through the cerebral cortex, the cerebral hemispheres control voluntary movements, sensory functions (hearing, smell, sight, touch and taste), the ability to speak and understand language, thinking, short and long-term memory, learning, attention and conscience; by means of the subcortical gray matter, moreover, they preside over functions such as the processing of emotions and memories, spatial memory, the consolidation of fear, motivated behaviors, decision-making aimed at a given reward (reward system) and, again, memory, learning and smell.

As can be seen, therefore, the cerebral hemispheres play a central role in mental-cognitive mechanisms and functions; all this, however, should not be surprising, because the brain of which they are part represents the most specialized portion of the entire brain.

Contralateral Organization of the Brain: What is it?

It has long been known that the right cerebral hemisphere controls the motor functions of the left half of the human body, while the left cerebral hemisphere controls the motor functions of the right half of the human body; the same is true for sensory information related to the sense of hearing and touch.

This curious functional feature of the cerebral hemispheres is what experts call the contralateral organization of the brain.

Cerebral Lateralization: What is it?

Also, in this case, there is now outdated evidence that the control centers of cognitive abilities reside in only one of the two cerebral hemispheres, either the right or the left; Using an example as an explanation, the language control centers take their place on the left cerebral hemisphere, while the cognitive faculties related to orientation in space belong to the right cerebral hemisphere.

This second functional peculiarity of the cerebral hemispheres is what experts define with the term "cerebral lateralization".

Effects in the clinical field of cerebral lateralization

Cerebral lateralization explains why injuries in one brain hemisphere have different consequences than injuries in the other hemisphere.

Functions of the Left-Brain Hemisphere

The left-brain hemisphere controls functions such as:

- The voluntary movements of the right side of the human body;
- The ability to articulate a speech and produce a written text. This ability resides in Broca's area;
- Understanding of language; this ability is shared between Broca's area and Wernicke's area;
- Logical reasoning;

- The calculation capacity. This ability takes place on the inferior parietal lobule of the parietal lobe;
- Analytical thinking.

Functions of the Right Brain Hemisphere

The right brain hemisphere, on the other hand, presides over the control of functions such as:

- The voluntary movements of the left side of the human body;
- The ability to identify objects;
- Spatial orientation;
- Creativity and imagination;
- The capacity for intuition;
- Intonation and emphasis in language.

Which Hemisphere of The Brain Do You Use Most?

Facts and mystifications about our "thinking organ"

How many times has it happened to you to find a quiz or something similar on the Net that claimed to be able to make you understand which hemisphere of the brain determined your way of being?

The importance attributed to this eventual response, in the common feeling, would in fact have implications on our personality. Many believe that people who use predominantly the left side of the brain should be more inclined to math and analytical science, while people who use the right side would have a natural inclination towards creativity.

But how much of this is true? As often happens, the most sensible answer is "only in part". While it's true that each of our hemispheres plays slightly different roles, individuals don't actually have a dominant side of the brain that governs their personality and abilities.

Rather, the research revealed that people use both hemispheres of the brain in virtually equal measure. However, what is true is that the left hemisphere of the brain is more related to the use of language, while the right hemisphere is more applied to the complexity of non-verbal communication.

Right versus Left

No, we do not want to go into the political arena, but simply to talk about the alleged dualism of the hemispheres of our brain. According to popular belief, everyone has a side of their brain that is dominant and determines personality, thoughts and behavior. Since people can be left-handed or right-handed, it is assumed that they can therefore also be dominated by one hemisphere instead of the other.

It is therefore said that people who mainly use the left side of the brain are more:

- analytical
- logical
- attentive to detail and oriented towards facts
- skilled with numbers
- predisposed to think using words

On the other hand, people with the predominant right hemisphere would be more:

- creative
- open to free thought

- able to see the big picture of things
- intuitive
- you are probably used to thinking in visualizations rather than words

What does the research tell us?

Recent research suggests that the left brain and right brain theory is incorrect. A 2013 study looked at three-dimensional images of more than 1,000 brains. On that occasion, the activity of both hemispheres was measured with the aid of an MRI scanner. The results obtained show that each person uses both hemispheres of the brain and that there does not appear to be a dominant side.

However, it turned out to be true that a person's brain activity differs depending on the task they are doing. For example, another study states that the language centers in the brain are located in the left hemisphere, while the right hemisphere is specialized for emotional and non-verbal communications.

The contribution made to research on the hemispheric specialization of cognitive functions led, for example, Roger W. Sperry, David Hunter Hubel and Torsten Nils Wiesel to win the Nobel Prize in 1981. However, popular cultural exaggeration around these discoveries has led to the development of beliefs about different personalities in relation to the preponderance of one hemisphere over the other.

Does hemispheric dominance differ from person to person?

The side of the brain used in every activity is not the same for every person. The side of the brain that is used for certain activities can be affected, for example, by whether a person is left-handed or right-handed. A 2014 study notes that up to 99% of right-handed individuals have language centers in the left side of the brain. But this is also the case for about 70% of left-handed people.

Hemispheric dominance varies from person to person also according to different activities. Science will need more research to fully understand all the factors that affect this aspect.

In conclusion

The theory that a person's personality is linked to the dominance of the left or right hemisphere of the brain is not supported by scientific research. Some people may believe that this theory is indeed in line with their attitudes. However, to understand the intricacies of this incredible organ, one should not rely on such impressions as much as one should use scientifically accurate models.

The common belief about the influence of hemispheres on our personality may have taken root so much because, in reality, brain activity is not symmetrical and varies from person to person.

Phantom Sensations – How Our Brain Processes the Sensation Of "Touch"

Have you ever had someone touch your left arm when they actually touched your right? Scientists know this phenomenon and call it phantom sensation: it can help shed light on how our brain reacts and processes the sensation of touch.

The human brain is still mysterious in many ways. There are complex phenomena that are beyond our understanding, such as phantom limb pain that occurs when a person believes they can detect pain or other tactile sensations in a limb that they have lost through amputation.

Some people experience tactile hallucinations during which they mistakenly believe they are experiencing a sensation when, in fact, no factor could have induced it. Tactile hallucinations usually occur in individuals who are under particular psychological conditions such as schizophrenia, but it is not uncommon for mentally and physically healthy individuals to experience similar phenomena.

For example, when a person is touched on the left hand, he may believe he has sensed a touch on his left foot or vice versa: this is precisely the case with what scientists call phantom sensation: researchers studying this strange situation are still a long way from understanding why this phenomenon occurs.

In a recent new study, the results of which appear published in Current Biology, a team of researchers from New York University and the Universities of Hamburg and Bielefeld, Germany, explain in detail what characterizes phantom sensations, arguing that a better understanding of this phenomenon could help specialists decipher other similar mysteries, including phantom limb pain. The limitations of previous explanations of how and where our brain processes process the sensation of touch become apparent when it comes to people who have had parts of their body amputated or who suffer from neurological diseases - notes study co-author Prof. Tobias Heed.

He points out that, to date, scientists have learned surprisingly little about how the human brain processes the sensation of touch.

People who have had a hand or leg amputated often report phantom sensations on those limbs - continues Prof. Heed -. But where exactly does this false perception come from?

Studying brain processes in depth

Until now, scientists thought that our conscious perception of where a touch occurred came from a topographical map stored in our brains. Following this hypothesis, parts of the body such as the hands, feet or face would be represented on this map.

However, this new study, which focused on behavioral analysis in fully healthy participants, indicates that the way the brain attributes tactile sensations is much more complicated.

In the current study, the researchers conducted five different experiments, each involving the collaboration of 12-20 healthy adults. During each experiment, participants agreed to have tactile stimulators attached to their hands and feet. The researchers used these stimulators to generate tactile sensations in two different parts of the body in quick succession and then asked the participants to report where they felt the touches. This type of test was then repeated several hundred times for each participant.

Surprisingly, in 8% of all cases, the subjects attributed the first touch to a part of the body that had not even been touched - giving us the opportunity to verify a fair distribution of the presence of phantom sensations - declares the lead researcher of the experiment, Stephanie Badde.

The 3 characteristics of phantom sensations

The previous conception, as we have mentioned, attributed the position of a touch dependent on maps of the body known to our brain: however, all this does not fit in any way with these new discoveries.

The study shows that phantom sensations can have 3 different characteristics:

The identity of the limb: a touch on one hand is felt by the other hand.

The side of the body: A person may think they feel a touch in their right hand when, in fact, it occurred on the right foot.

The normal anatomical position of the limb (right or left). For example, if a person crosses their arms or legs, placing the right limb to the left of the body, they may mistakenly perceive a touch to the right arm as a touch to the left foot.

When parts of the body are placed on the other side, for example when we cross our legs, the two-coordinate systems conflict - continues Prof. Heed.

Current findings do not just contradict previous understanding of how the brain processes the perception of touch, but how, in the future, they help guide research into phantom limb sensations and other related phenomena.

A fascinating mystery that opens up new doors for us to learn more about our thinking organ.

BRAIN, CREATIVITY AND WELLNESS

Creative thinking becomes mental and physical well-being as it is proposed as a valid alternative to excluding negative thoughts that limit the ability to explore the inner world and also allows you to make full use of the multifaceted brain capacities with the relative benefit.

Creativity of thought frees you from malaise precisely in that it frees the mind from acquired conditioning; this is particularly important in every occasion in which a psychic and mental maturation is needed. In fact, following changes that occur in everyone's life, some problems often become unsolvable precisely because of the failure of every attempt aimed at seeking solutions on the basis of obsolete mental schemes and behaviors, rather than trying to creatively re-read the contingent situation.

These considerations make us understand the importance of knowing the basic functioning of the brain structure so as to avoid failure due to not being able to remove that intellectual opacity and mental crystallization that generate negative thinking and consequently psycho-physical discomfort.

Structure of the brain

The brain is divided into two main sections, Right and Left, which in evolution have been particularly differentiated by modifying the neuronal infrastructures of the Upper Cerebral Hemispheres.

This division of the brain into two sections reflects the fact that our body also has a binary joint: in fact we have two eyes, two ears, two holes in the nose, a tongue that differentiates sweet from salty ... two hands, two legs and so on.

The cerebral hemispheres

This suggests that the functions of the brain, as an expression of a thinking activity, are also double, and this means that we can mean what we observe through two alternative and complementary modalities: the one logical-rational (i.e. sequential, analytical, deductive) and the other intuitive-holistic (i.e. synthetic, globalizing, inductive) which basically correspond to the functionally differentiated procedures of the activities of the two cerebral hemispheres.

It is important to understand how these two ways of thinking can be correctly coordinated to acquire different levels and styles of thinking, without generating contradictions that internally lead to dangerous splits of awareness in the construction of one's own creative personality.

From the studies of FMR (Functional Magnetic Resonance) the different functionality of the two cerebral hemispheres is interpreted as a dual ability to correlate the Long-Term Memory (LTM) with the Short-Term Storage (STM) processes from which the greater or greater less ability and speed of action / reaction of thought.

Thought is in fact determined by the flow of memory activities that use different relationship patterns between MLT and MBT, which interpose the old and the new flow of information circulating between the external world and our physiological brain ability.

<u>Left hemisphere</u>: formal logical modalities to simplify the complexity of information

The logical-rational functionality of the Left Hemisphere develops by activating the associative capacity of the Wernike Area which tends to facilitate integration with the MLT.

It is the area of the brain that is crucial for understanding language. People who have neurophysiological damage in that area do not understand the meaning of the words and are unable to express themselves. It was so named because it was discovered by Carl Wernike in 1874.

The logical-significant operation is essentially based on the combination of four logical-formal operators that correspond in spoken language to: <YES, NO, AND, OR> which are used to analyze and combine the complex dynamics of the flow in terms of simpler units of information. The YES makes the flow of thought proceed and the AND allows you to connect a section or image acquired with a subsequent one, while the NO interrupts the flow of thought and diverts it towards an alternative selected by OR.

<u>REWIRE your BRAIN</u>

This Logical Thinking Mode attributable to the predominance of the activities of the Left Hemisphere of the Brain, directs the attention and the feasible comparison in terms of recognition and identity, with the past acquired experience of LTM (long-term memory). Logical thinking, through its analytical operators, has the ability to discover the best way to combine sections of the information flow by separating it, selecting it and combining the chosen sections and finally generating an extension capable of determining a prediction on what to do; in this way it becomes possible to solve complex problems by means of a meaningful processing of the information flow (PROBLEM - SOLVING). Certainly, this methodology contains the risk of consolidating one's own ways of thinking by systematically activating the brain areas that allow the result of a logical reflection to be combined in the best way, but in fact this does not allow the brain in its functional entirety to intuitively reorganize the information. overall through parallel paths more typical of the Right Hemisphere's ways of thinking.

Right Hemisphere and Lateral Thinking to modify the logical-interpretative schemes

This allows us to become aware of the limits of logical-formal thinking and therefore facilitates the ability to develop the parallel activities of LATERAL THINKING in order to AVOID ERRORS even BEFORE SOLVING THEM (PROBLEM - SAVING).

The psychologist Edward De Bono identifies four important factors that suggest an attitude aimed at using lateral thinking in a synergistic and complementary way: 1) in order to recognize and modify the dominant criteria and ideas, 2) which polarize the perception of a problem, 3) and prevent us from looking for different ways of looking at things, 4) and therefore from loosening the rigid control of logical-linear thinking to encourage the development of creativity.

Creativity is therefore within reach for each of us. In fact being creative does not depend exclusively on genetics, precisely because genes are not able to manage the physical and mental changes that occur over a lifetime.

Creativity is therefore the way of knowing how to use the plasticity of the brain to respond to the complexity of events, putting into operation the multiple and articulated intellectual functions that each of us is genetically endowed with.

As a block of marble takes the shape conceived by the sculptor's creativity, so the brain of each of us can be empowered by ourselves, consciously improving the intellectual functions, and thus acquiring a well-being deriving from the confidence in one's natural creative abilities. Remember that becoming creative does not just mean inventing something new or being original by force, but essentially it means finding satisfaction in making the most of both the developmental potential of your brain.

THE EIGHT OF INFINITY, MORE THAN A SIMPLE BRAIN GYM EXERCISE

Cristian Dillinger studied sports and movement sciences at the University of Graz, Austria. He is a Touch for Health instructor, a Hyperton X lecturer and a member of the International Faculty of the Educational Kinesiology Foundation for Austria. In his studio he practices cranio-sacral therapy according to Upledger, visceral manipulation according to Barral and educational physiotherapy (Guided Affective Imagery). He is the President of the Association of Professional Kinesiology of Austria (OBK) and the director of the Moving Institute in Graz

The eight of infinity is more than just a Brain Gym exercise

The infinity symbol is a mathematical symbol

The letter X has turned into a knot

The crossing point of two arches

A symmetrical toy race track that changes direction by making a left turn, crossing itself to make a right turn.

Crossing the visual midline

Two connected wedding rings symbolizing the marriage bond

The eight Tibetans stimulate the free flow of energy

Shoelaces symbolize support in movement

A tuxedo bow tie for the opera ball

A symbol for the connection and collaboration between the two hemispheres of the brain

A symbol for the connection and collaboration between the right and left sides of the body addresses all areas of the brain involving the complete visual field

Many images accompany us (sometimes symbolically) when we draw the eight of infinity. We can encounter this form in various contexts, particularly when a two-part connection is involved with the crossing of the auditory, kinesthetic and visual midline. A kinesiological rebalancing aims at the collaboration between the two hemispheres and the two sides of the body; at the same time, it focuses on the physical integration of the goal, which is reinforced by the eight of infinity. Six pairs of muscles, behind the eyeballs, direct the gaze of the eyes in different directions, and cause the eyes to focus, in a synchronized way, on a common target. Activities that precede a kinesiological rebalancing can highlight when the eyes are out of sync. While one eye focuses the lens, the other does not cooperate. In stressful situations, it appears that only one eye can handle the situation by processing visual information related to stress, while the other eye does not participate.

The eight of infinity perfectly trains the coordination of the two eyes

The eight of the infinite puts in contact and connects two systems; it has no beginning or end, so it reinforces a continuous flow of movement. The figure eight supports the integration of letters into the flow of the word, improving the cooperation of both eyes, arms and hands, and makes it possible to reflect on words, between the left and right hemisphere.

A phenomenon: a look at a person's inner organization

Phenomenon: the boy looks at the image only with his right eye. The 'forced catch' is a sign of unilateral compensation.

Watching a phenomenon manifest itself is a real revelation. When we see a child draw an eight of infinity, we can observe different characteristics related to the coordination of movement.

We enter the heart of different stages of evolutionary development. Has a child who has been certified mature enough for school really achieved the cognitive skills that allow him to interpret words satisfactorily in order to perform the required tasks? Are the child's fine motor skills developed to the point of allowing him to learn to write? And enough to allow him to carry out the task of writing? Does he possess sufficient perception to be able to process numbers?

By watching a child draw the infinity symbol, we can perfectly observe his state of coordination, as well as his state of development of explicit (declarative) and implicit (procedural) memory. Our kinesiological experience teaches us that we can support this development by applying the exercises of the eight of infinity.

School skills: reading, writing and counting can be reinforced by the eight of infinity

Movement coordination: how do we organize our movements and actions?

The exercise consists in drawing an eight of infinity without stopping. The pupil turns the sheet in the wrong direction and in this way it becomes impossible to draw the eight of infinity on the whole sheet. We can assume that there is a problem crossing the visual midline. The thumb is very stiff which indicates that the student is using the "wrong" hand to write. There is no flow in the movement.

The coordination of movement and the order and organization of motor actions oriented towards a specific goal or purpose. (Mainel 1977)

The order means, in this context, the congruence of all the motor parameters in the respective situation.

In the case of reading, writing and arithmetic, this corresponds to the ability to understand, express, sense of space and abstraction of numbers. Let 's examine the concept of motor coordination in relation to the school competences listed above taking into account the state of development based on age.

Age-appropriate motor coordination is defined as harmonious and highly efficient collaboration of muscles, nerves and senses, which results in balanced motor actions, as well as rapid reactions, in response to specific situations (motor reflexes) - Kiphart 1982.

Considering the above tasks, a student must have developed certain skills in order to perform school skills.

The term "coordinative characteristics" was coined to make specific traits within the multiplicity of different motor aspects more understandable.

Which of these characteristics are important for a person to be able to read, write and calculate easily? There are other features besides these five listed.

Rhythm of movement: in order to attribute meaning to written, read and spoken words, it is necessary to have a certain individual rhythm, such as intonation in speaking.

Flow of movement: need to connect / form syllables and words to understand what you are reading, writing or reciting.

Movement speed: gradually increase the speed to arrive at a smooth reading, a smooth writing and an adequate speed in performing the calculations.

Accuracy of movement: every single word, within a sentence, is properly aligned and is legible, both for the writer and for the reader. The rules of order and orientation are recognizable.

Consistency of movement: the size and breadth of the letters become more constant with age and maturity. This helps an organizational model; constant shapes can be created and represented. The corrections, initially exaggerated, resulting in an irregular handwriting, become less evident; the movement becomes more harmonious and uniform.

Fine motor skills develop first in females. Males have a tendency to acquire writing skills by involving shoulder and arm muscles, rather than using finger and wrist movements. This appears to be a more difficult way to acquire writing skills, because the movements starting from the large joints of the upper body cannot be coordinated as precisely as those starting from the fingers and wrist.

The development of reading and writing skills

"Negative transfer" in changing the directions of the curves. The right curve is anticipated and "disturbs", so it is not possible to draw a curve to the left first.

In the initial phase of reading, the child's forefinger glides along the line and guides the eyes in the passage from letter to letter. In the second stage, the eyes draw the line without the help of the finger. The child gradually learns to understand whole words. To do this, the child must have developed the ability to create a mental image of syllables or whole words; moreover, he must possess a spatial perception in order to understand numbers and proportions.

The eight of infinity, drawn by the pupils in the projects I led at school, show that those children, declared ready for schooling, were not able to draw an eight of infinity correctly even after six months of school. This indicates that this type of movement is not yet fixed and stored in the motor memory area of the brain.

Sometimes it can be observed that the movement of the eight of infinity can be successfully completed several times in a row, but not with the same consistency and quality: this means that continuous practice is required.

Styles and learning channels: visual / auditory / kinesthetic

The eight of infinity drawn with the wrong hand and with closed eyes highlights the evolutionary state, the inner representation of movement in childhood memory.

The eight of infinity can take different forms: some are more voluminous, others are thin, still others asymmetrical. From the way in which an eight of infinity is drawn, it can be concluded which sense is most involved.

According to Neuro-Linguistic Programming, looking up means that the visual channel has been activated; looking from left to right and vice versa instead, the auditory canal is activated; finally, looking below the horizontal midline stimulates the kinesthetic canal. If the intersection of the eight of infinity is below the midline, the student has used the visual channel. A symmetrical and harmonious eight indicates use of the auditory canal, while large circles below the midline suggest activation of the kinesthetic canal.

Considering all this, it could be concluded that the eight of infinity reveals the preferred perceptual channel of the moment and could indicate the person's learning style in general.

"Break the brain"

In one of my school projects, pupils have to repeat the movement continuously on a sheet of paper in an infinite flow, like on a toy car track. From the position of the hand and fingers holding the pencil, I can deduce if they write with the dominant hand. The expressive hemisphere, which is basically responsible for writing and expression, is located on the opposite side of the head from the writing hand. However, we can find a compensatory position of the hand, which normally appears in left-handed people when they write with their right hand: in this case, the expressive brain is on the same side as the writing hand, and the hand appears as a hook (the wrist is inverted), or the thumb is particularly extended at its base.

In the past, left-handers were often forced to use the right hand: this constraint, in Anglo-Saxon countries, was called "breaking the brain".

Visual preference

The first eight of infinity was drawn with open eyes implying the visual channel; the subsequent ones were drawn with eyes closed. The visual perceptual system is unable to maintain control. There is not enough mental representation in memory, especially with regards to spatial memory, to cross the midline. By working with both sides of the brain and body one is able to create an inner image of movement.

One can easily imagine how difficult it is to maintain the connection between the left hemisphere and the right hemisphere under such stress.

The more the student becomes involved in this constraint, the more difficult it becomes for him to bring out his full potential in terms of his academic skills.

The eight of infinity is a wonderful tool in human history for performance improvement: a tool that gives access to the flow of life. It is certainly no coincidence that it has been adopted by kinesiology as a strong tool to bring out the potential.

How to Develop the Right Brain Hemisphere? Exercises for Non-Symmetry

There are rarely people in whom the work of the hemispheres is absolutely synchronous, that is, most of them have the asymmetry of the cerebral hemispheres.

People whose two hemispheres work in equal parts, in the same way, can make the most of their mental potential: they become geniuses with excellent memory, with the ability to analyze everything that happens, with excellent attention. It turns out that with the help of a few exercises, almost everyone can get close to the ideal - synchronous work.

Development of both cerebral hemispheres

Make sure you read longer articles, pick up a book or read a magazine or newspaper. We are the generation that skims content and this weakens our left brain. You can even read about your favorite topic, such as web design, graphics, advertising, or copy. The key is that you read, don't look.

Both lobes of the brain are completely different when considering their actions. Both lobes are essential to ensure a balanced life. However, in nature, one side of the brain can be stronger than the other. Children are no different. As the brain grows, children tend to show noticeable differences between the two brain lobes. While the left side is important for school and academic activities, the right side is important for other things. For optimal life performance, parents should try to educate their children to develop both sides of the brain.

Soviet scientists in their time conducted a very interesting and curious experiment, based on the temporary closure of one hemisphere. This was done using an electric current.

The charge was applied to one hemisphere, while the other remained active. With the help of these studies, it was possible to reliably find out what each hemisphere of the brain is responsible for.

It may seem very complicated. However, a concerted effort will help you achieve your goals. Here are some simple tips to teach your kids how to brainstorm. The art of all brain training is quite difficult because you will be dealing with two different brain lobes, each with their own specialties and abilities.

Whole Brain Study is a general neural development system, which improves the neural connections between the two lobes of the brain. Eventually this will lead to the creation of a much stronger and more reliable pathway for neural thinking. Whole Brain Learning is not just about class and academic performance. It also deals with a number of other skills and abilities in addition to academic skills. A favorable brain is one that works best in any condition, including academic, social, logical, and psychological ones.

Areas of responsibility of the cerebral hemispheres

In medicine, there are concepts such as a left-brain or right-brain person. They indicate that one of a person's two hemispheres works best. This can only affect his behavior, appearance, intellectual abilities, etc.

According to Soviet scientific research, it can be said that a healthy person is a person who has both hemispheres functioning and it does not matter which one is better. When one of the hemispheres was turned off, some defects in language and behavior were observed.

To improve social skills, you may need to include activities to help your children learn how to make the right choice, plan and decide, and become independent in life. Most children who are gifted with the right hemisphere are quite poor in expressing themselves in front of other people. Here are some activities that improve left brain abilities.

Sit down with your child and play a game. Help the others create simple words and syllables. Explain the meaning of the words in a simple way ... If possible, ask them to use the words in simple sentences. Example. If the word "please" is created, ask your children to use that word in the sentence. An example could read like this: "Please give me a cup of milk."

For example, when working only with the left hemisphere, it was noticed that a person becomes talkative, enters a conversation well, his vocabulary is fully revealed, that is, the ability to think during speech has been preserved. At the same time, the speech itself became nasal, confused, and the person from a potential great interlocutor turned into someone who was even unpleasant to hear.

Discussion and exchange of ideas: a discussion on a specific topic is a great tool for learning to speak in front of others. When someone is discussing or exchanging ideas, they can use their brain functions to express themselves so that everyone understands their mind. Debate is also stressful and can eradicate the fear of being on stage.

Role play: role play increases trust and social interaction between young children. Provide a topic for creating an RP session. This could be a post office session where one of your children will be the Post Master and the others will be customers looking for some service.

Without the functioning of the right hemisphere, a person loses the ability to recognize various intonations, melodies, the brain does not process the information that comes to him in the correct way. In addition, if a person's right hemisphere is turned off, he will not be able to perform even the simplest tasks, such as collecting the same from multiple figures. His sense of time and space is disturbed, he can forget a lot of what he knew well.

Creativity is the cornerstone of life. Without creativity, people would be like walking and breathing vegetables. Furthermore, creativity is a tool for creating something unique and special. Right-brained children are very creative and can create simple things out of thin air. On the other hand, children of the left hemisphere are quite poor in this area.

Modeling Clay: Modeling clay is perhaps the oldest brain augmentation activity in history. Clay modeling optimizes creative functional areas of the brain such as imagination, imaging, a holistic approach and hand-eye coordination. When your kids play with models and clay, their finger movements become stronger, which is a basic need for creativity. To be creative and artistic, very young children in the age group 3 to 6 need to develop correct hand movements, especially the thumbs.

But at the same time, a left hemisphere functioning allows a person to think logically, that is, it is responsible only for logic. The subjects were asked to assemble logical chains and they succeeded perfectly. At the same time, a person cannot name even the simplest objects that a small child knows.

The right hemisphere of the brain is responsible for creating new ideas, the ability to predict a certain situation. But when the left hemisphere is turned off, all thoughts and ideas remain within a person, because his speech is significantly disturbed. However, the right hemisphere allows you to grasp the pitch and be a good listener in a conversation. Such a person has no logical thinking.

Stronger fingers means they are able to hold objects correctly without any unstable movement. All painters and sculptors have very strong and stable fingers and toes. Experts suggest that young children should collect grass from the back garden to strengthen their fingers and movements. Holding a pen or pencil will also help them learn and master their fingers and hands. Drawing and painting with different subjects such as pencil, oil paints and watercolors will help them understand the main differences between colors and their combinations.

Only the work of both hemispheres helps a person to exist normally in a natural environment. Apparently, even with a simple communication with a person, the interlocutor must clearly express his thoughts and understand what they are saying, be sure to capture the intonations.

Let them draw what they want and color it too. With this activity, they can see the world as a whole. Imagination is another positive that comes naturally to these children. Give them models of different things and ask them to refer to natural objects.

How to prepare the brain for exercise

Language skills come naturally for the remaining intelligent children. Conversely, children with left brains are quite poor on this side. The most important task is to prepare your children in the field of communication and basic language acquisition.

Every simple daily action requires a certain algorithm and, without a functioning hemisphere, it will be interrupted. For example, a person goes to the bread shop. This common everyday situation requires a preparatory algorithm, yet none of us think about it.

Meanwhile, a person needs to get dressed, take a certain amount of money with them, leave the apartment, go down to the first floor and at the same time know exactly where, in which direction and in which shop to go, and also remember that they need thebread ... A seemingly simple situation is impossible without the work of the two cerebral hemispheres.

Exercises for non-symmetry

Dialogue and communication are the two most important activities. Make sure you talk to your children every day to improve their language skills. Communication comes easily to those children who develop the ability to speak by speaking to others with confidence and courage. Take the topic and start a dialogue. Make sure your kids talk more than you do. They should ask questions and answer your questions. In this way oral skills will also be refined. Offer them a drawing contest by asking for a specific topic.

From his behavior, a person can assume which of the hemispheres works worse and which is better. In order for the two hemispheres to work synchronously, it is necessary to revive the one that works less efficiently. The synchronization of the cerebral hemispheres, according to many psychologists, involves hard work on oneself.

Exercises to synchronize the work of both hemispheres

Various psychological techniques have developed many simple exercises to improve the symmetry of the hemispheres. They are usually used by young children who want to develop certain talents in themselves. But they are perfect for any age group.

They should be able to draw some pictures and write their explanations under each picture. Signs and symbols for reading and teaching in school are other exercises to strengthen the left brain.

Spatial relations and movements.

Spatial relationships are an amazing skill for the brain. On the other hand, spatial movement is an offshoot of spatial relationships and can improve proper brain power. Children who are strong in this skill are able to sufficiently analyze various bits of information and create significant spatial coherence.

Implement various activities to enhance this special mental strength.

Elbows and knees - while standing and keeping straight, perform alternating touches with the left elbow of the right knee and the right elbow of the left knee. By doing these physical things, a person will force the work of the two hemispheres to align with a certain synchronicity. Also, this exercise has analogues, for example, you can sit on the floor, keeping your back straight and alternately touch your toes with the opposite hand

Ring: quickly and neatly fold the fingers on one hand, forming them into a ring, and it is better to do it back and forth (from the thumb to the little finger and back)

Nose – ear - grasp the nose with the left hand and the left ear with the right. So, at the same time, let go, clap your hands and change over. These exercises are also called "cross", they help perfectly synchronize the work of the left and right hemisphere;

Circles: stand on your left leg and with your right try to draw a circle on the floor, first clockwise and then counterclockwise. Then do the same but swapping legs. It should be noted that with such exercises both hemispheres are maximally involved, because the leg on which the person is standing is the supporting one, and drawing circles with the foot is a completely sequential action. Both lower limbs function at the same time, and therefore two hemispheres

various coordination exercises (jumps on one leg with alternating legs, squats with knees extended forward, etc.)

Figures: stand up, straighten your back and draw figures in the air with your hand. The shapes should be different, for example, the left hand draws a circle and the right hand draws a rhombus at the same time. The synchronization of actions with the hands in this case is a step towards the synchronization of the work of the cerebral hemispheres.

Based on the mentioned exercises, a person can come up with many similar ones and perform them every day, if he has set himself the task of adapting the work of the cerebral hemispheres and using its potential to the maximum.

Anchoring movements such as twisting, bending, swinging arms and picking up objects from the ground are some of the simple activities that will help your kids in many ways. Running, jumping, and walking are other activities that can improve spatial thinking. Teach your children how to act on the directions.

Give them some directions and follow them; this activity will help them learn symbols and decipher hidden codes and meanings. Brain exercises for whole brain development occur in many shapes and patterns. However, what you want to use will depend on what exactly you want from your kids. In many cases, parents want to improve right-sided brain because it is associated with better academic and learning outcomes in school.

To achieve this, it is also very useful to perform other synchronized actions, such as trying to juggle at least two objects. If juggling is difficult, you can sign up for piano lessons.

The great pianists could boast the synchronicity of both hemispheres, because playing the piano causes maximum symmetry. If a person loves music and wants to open up in this environment, an accordion or accordion is also perfect for synchronization.

Focusing on just one area of the brain can be counterproductive. If your child has a strong left brain, you will have to work very hard to improve the other side. Indeed, these children always pose a serious problem for their parents.

Try left brain versus right brain mental crunch

The functions of the brain are clearly separated, aimed at performing various functions. Each hemisphere needs a special approach and therefore they need to be developed in different ways.

The challenge of each hemisphere

Let's see what each of the hemispheres is responsible for. The left hemisphere is logic, literal perception of information, math skill, writing, reading, language skill.

Try painting a vase instead of a face or vice versa. Align and compare relationships with the other side of the drawing. This time the left brain might win, but why not try the exercise again and see what happens. We can train our mind so that many behaviors and thought processes are well-established habits and it may take a little longer to learn how to access the right brain, but you can.

The left hemisphere is responsible for building causal relationships. Thus, we understand that left brain thinking is inherently quite rational. Now let's move on to thinking about the right hemisphere, which is more spontaneous and irrational.

The instruction to name different parts of your face meant that you were forced to actually use your left brain. Then you were asked to complete the second half of the drawing symmetrically. However, this can only be done by inserting the visual spatial side of the brain into the right hand. This is the part of the brain that, without even knowing it, evaluates the relationships of sizes, curves, angles and shapes.

Experience the transition from the left brain to the right brain

We have deliberately created a number of conditions that create a conflict between the left hemisphere and the right brain to make you feel this. The difficulty of making this change creates a sense of conflict and confusion - at times it feels like instant paralysis. However, by learning how to appeal to the right brain, you can learn how to trick the left brain to leave you alone to continue drawing with the right brain, the side of the brain that really knows how to draw.

The right hemisphere is responsible for imagination, emotions, musical ability, visual arts. Among the many talented and creative people we all know well, there are many left-handed people, that is, people with dominant right brain thinking.

These are, for example, Mozart, Leonardo da Vinci, Raphael and many others. Furthermore, the right hemisphere is responsible for intuition and imaginative thinking.

So, having figured out what the right hemisphere is for, let's move on to how we can develop it. Of course, one way is to simply use the left side of the body, the one it controls.

That is, you can start by using your left hand more, for example, when brushing your teeth, eating, washing dishes, etc. Some recommend learning to write with your left hand. However, it is important to understand that the abuse of this type of action can negatively affect your psyche, up to the development of epilepsy.

Therefore, it is recommended to use "safer" methods. The first is to learn how to play a musical instrument. When a person plays on something, he uses both hands - left and right, which is precisely what contributes to the development of the right hemisphere in right-handers, and of the left in left-handers.

Also, a kind of brain hemispheres training is text typing and other similar actions. Now consider the second exercise: reading the words from the end, i.e. if you need to read the word "red", read it as "der". This can be done with any text.

Speaking of colors: it will also be a good exercise for the right hemisphere if you have in front of the words that represent one color, while they themselves will be written in a different color, and you will not pronounce the words themselves, but the color in which they are written.

For example, you have the word "red" which is written in green ... You will have to say the word "green". At first glance it is simple, but not everyone can do it quickly.

Another effective exercise - touch the tip of the nose with the index finger of the right hand, and with the left - to the right knee. Then clap your hands and do the opposite, eg. with the left hand, touch the tip of the nose and with the right finger touch the left knee. And do it whenever you have time. That said, try to do it as quickly as possible.

You have to learn not only to empathize with other people, but to look at the world through their eyes, so a person is deeply in touch with the reality of other people.

You need to learn to draw, perceive the world around you in an abstract way, to begin with you can become a designer of your apartment, take a picture, trust your intuition when choosing a color scheme.

A person needs to often listen to soothing music, during which he can relax, collect his thoughts, direct creative energy in the right direction.

And with the simultaneous work of both hands (drawing, text on a computer, playing musical instruments), both hemispheres are included in the work, which means that the brain develops effectively.

As you move, touch the knee of the left leg with the left hand and touch the right leg with the right. Increase the number of times with each workout. It is important to follow the rhythm, while it is necessary to look at a drawing with 2 parallel lines, which must be placed at eye level.

For the next exercise, you need to take a comfortable position, either standing or sitting. At the same time, you can draw a drawing with your own hands, on paper or in the air, always with a mirror reflection of the hand.

Exercises for non-symmetry

The exercise is performed similarly to the first symmetrical, but the hands should touch the opposite knee, right hand - left knee.

To develop the right hemisphere, it is necessary to regularly perform finger gymnastics, you can perform such exercises: straighten the index finger of the right hand and left thumb. Then straighten the index finger of the left hand and the thumb with the right in a mirror. Over time, it is necessary to increase the pace.

EXERCISES FOR THE BRAIN

While they are not usually two elements that we connect, monotony is detrimental to our ability to concentrate. For this reason, one of the best brain exercises is to add new activities to your everyday routine

With age, stress and worries, the mind deteriorates and stops functioning as it did when you were young. If this is your case, if you are in the period of exams, you are plagued by anxiety or the passing years are starting to be felt, we recommend some exercises for the brain.

Before explaining what, they consist of, we need to understand how our head works. As you know, our brain has two hemispheres, the left and the right, and each of them has different functions.

The left hemisphere, in fact, deals with verbal activities and logical analysis. The right hemisphere, on the other hand, manages all the non-verbal part and creativity.

For this reason, the best exercises for the brain are the ones that connect the two hemispheres.

1. Brain gym

Brain gym helps keep your brain fit

These mental gymnastics help to enhance creativity, concentration and psychomotor skills and, in addition, facilitates learning.

Sociologist Paul Dennison proposes a series of brain exercises consisting of 26 simple body movements that help connect the two hemispheres. We recommend that you precede the brain gym exercises with a little warm-up, chest breathing and drinking some water. The ideal would be to do these exercises every day, repeating each exercise 10 times for 30 seconds.

2. Cross crawl exercise

To do this exercise, you need to lift your right knee and, at the same time, bring your left elbow closer to the knee. Then return to the starting position and repeat the same movement with the opposite limbs. You may be wondering what this exercise has to do with the brain?

This simple exercise optimizes the balance of the activity of our nervous system, which improves psychomotor skills and concentration, which are necessary above all to work on one's creativity.

3. Remember phone numbers

Memorizing phone numbers is one of the best brain exercises. Unlike the first two exercises, this one requires only a little mental effort. Analyze your diary and select the phone numbers you use most often. After that, try to remember them by heart. Do this exercise every day and you will see that your brain will start to be much more receptive the moment it has to memorize something. Memory is a part of our brain activity necessary to develop important aspects such as creativity, since we humans are able to imagine only starting from what we already know.

4. Listen to music

An enjoyable activity like listening to music can turn into your best ally against stress and an excellent companion during your study hours. In this context, the research of Dr. Tomatis stands out, who demonstrated that Mozart's music helps in therapies against depression. This is how the "Mozart effect" was born, that is a current of psychological and musical studies according to which the rhythm and melodies created by this composer favor oxygenation of the brain. The result is better concentration, which makes this activity a great exercise for the brain.

5. Escaping monotony is one of the best exercises for the brain

Escape from monotony.

Doing the same things every day causes the brain to relax and, therefore, decreases the levels of attention. In this way, we only damage our ability to concentrate. Taking this information into consideration, one of the best brain exercises is to change your way home or to open up to new ways of socializing. In fact, meeting new people helps to connect the two hemispheres of the brain, which is particularly interesting. On the one hand, in fact, intuition and curiosity are awakened and, at the same time, we put logic and our verbal skills into practice.

6.   Don't always put things in the same place

For the same reasons that we have listed in the previous point, always putting your objects in the same place facilitates the appearance of automatisms which, of course, reduces our levels of attention.

If, on the other hand, we move some object inside our home, we will have to think about its new location, memorize it and remember it, which is equivalent to an intense gym session for our mind, without the need for anything other than ourselves and our home.

Breathing Exercise to Harmonize the Cerebral Hemispheres

Facilitating the connection between the two hemispheres has long been the interest of many disciplines, especially those dealing with breathing and its role. Breathing supplies the blood with oxygen and blood nourishes the brain, which is why any type of stimulating breathing should contribute to the health of our hemispheres, without distinction. We have every interest in facilitating communication between the two hemispheres, to take full advantage of all our abilities.

There are various types of breathing that favor this stimulation, here is one whose particular role is to contribute to the balance of the cerebral hemispheres, calm the mind and rebalance the yin and yang in the body.

- Breathe while standing or sitting, with eyes closed.
- Place the middle finger and index finger of the right hand in the center of the forehead, between the eyebrows.
- Imagine that the nose is a roof whose top is located at the level of the forehead, below the middle and index fingers.

- Place the thumb on the right nostril and the ring finger on the left nostril.
- With your thumb, close the right nostril and leave the left open.
- Breathe in the air through the left nostril, make it rise along the nasal canal and direct it towards the top, ie under the index and middle fingers gently resting in the middle of the forehead.
- When the air has reached the top, open the right nostril by removing the thumb that closed it and plug the left nostril with the ring finger.
- Let the air flow back down the nasal canal to the right, outwards. In this way, the air has traveled the two sides of the roof passing from the top.
- Now, inhale to the right, blocking the left nostril and direct the air towards the top. Close the right nostril and release the left, letting the air flow back down the channel through the left nostril, then repeat.
- Continue the exercise until you feel a peace of mind taking hold within you.

Training Your Mind: 12 Exercises You Can Do Every Day

A couple of months ago, the owners of a popular mind-training app were fined a few million dollars for telling their customers they were going to get smarter.

The reason? Misleading Advertising: There is no scientific study in the world that shows that you can get smarter. Neither with their App, nor with other systems.

So, what's the point of doing brain exercises?

Is training the mind any good?

Well, from the point of view of brain aging, the first scientific evidence is beginning to emerge that training the mind can delay deterioration. And this is already very good news, even if unfortunately, it is not that the results are exceptional.

From a brain-boosting point of view, little or nothing is known, and that's why the founders of the App got their fine.

However, I believe that, in evaluating the effectiveness of brain training, an interesting analogy can be made with memory techniques: in fact, applying them does not increase your memory at all, but your ability to memorize. Which are two different things.

If before studying memory techniques you were perhaps able, with your "natural" abilities, to read and remember for a few seconds a number of at most 8-10 digits (and that's already a lot!), After studying them your "natural" memory continues to be able to remember 8-10 digits maximum. So, your memory hasn't increased. But if you use the memory technique of phonetic conversion, your ability to memorize numbers easily reaches 20 or 30 digits, and even more. Now, in my opinion, more or less the same thing applies to the other brain faculties. I don't think they can be increased in an absolute sense, at least not with the current scientific resources we possess.

Because intelligence in an absolute sense is complex, difficult both to define and to measure. You can understand "improve it"!

But we can certainly use the skills we already have much better. That is, "maybe we can't get smarter, but we can certainly use our brains better."

But how do you train your mind?

From a logistical point of view, it's much easier than going to the gym.

In fact, you can train your mind at any time and in any place, with a practically infinite variety of tools: yourself and the world around you.

1. Write with your non-dominant hand

That is, with the left if you are right-handed and with the right if you are left-handed. Trying every now and then to write (by hand, not on a computer) with the "wrong" hand, stimulates synaptic activity in your brain (synapses are structures that allow communication between nerve cells) that are not normally used.

And it does it massively: writing is in fact an extremely complex activity, which involves many brain areas, from those of language to those of fine control of the movement of the fingers.

Furthermore, to write with the "wrong" hand you will also need a surplus of mental focus, which is not normally needed when using the "good" hand.

2. Take a shower with your eyes closed

Sight is a very powerful sense, in fact the most powerful when it comes to using memory; however, we use it so much that it eventually "turns off" all the other senses a bit. And since each of our senses refers to specific brain areas, if a sense is used little, its reference brain area is also activated little.

By taking a shower with your eyes closed you will be able to focus better on the tactile sensations given by the water, and by the sponge; as you will be more sensitive to smells coming from soap and the sound of water near your ears.

Plus, you'll relax like hell!

3. Recognize objects by touch

Kindergarten children often play a game in which they have to recognize objects, with their eyes closed, touching them only with their hands. Thus, they find themselves evaluating with touch things that they normally recognize with their eyes, in particular the texture and shape of objects. To recognize an object in this way, the brain has to make many comparisons and analogies with previous experiences, very different from those it does using sight.

Furthermore, the uncertainty about what is being touched and the playful character of the task give this exercise an emotional content that positively affects brain activation.

4. Play with numbers

It is a classic but always valid way to train the mind. For example, you can count backwards, so as to stimulate the brain by making it do something normal (counting), but in an unusual way.

Or make multiplications in the mind between two-digit numbers, so that in carrying out the operation you are forced to create "reports" that the brain must remember, and then add them at the end.

5.   Look at objects in reverse

Visual memory is powerful and very useful, even for studying; but it takes little to deceive her, and by deceiving her you stimulate her a little.

Take everyday objects and observe them after putting them upside down; your brain will certainly recognize the object in question, i.e. the usual pattern of shapes and colors that identify it, but it will also notice a number of different relationships of the object with its surroundings, as well as new and interesting details that it has already seen, but on which he has never dwelled before,

You know the expression "looking at things from another point of view?". By doing this exercise you will find that it really means something.

6.   Taste, and above all, smell

Marcel Proust begins his 2,000-page masterpiece "In Search of Lost Time" starting from the memories that suddenly emerge when he tastes a madeleine (a French biscuit). Good grief, two thousand pages of a book triggered by the taste of a biscuit!

The brain structures connected to our olfactory and gustatory receptors are part of the oldest and "primitive" area of our nervous system, and are largely adjacent to the hippocampus, which is considered the true brain center of memory (and partly of emotions)

The anatomical proximity between these structures is also reflected in some functional correlations much studied in neurology: everyone knows by now that the memory capacity of taste and smell, even if it is not as detailed as the visual one, is not only very powerful, but also associated strongly with emotions.

Furthermore, particularly as regards the sense of smell, we have an enormous, innate ability to distinguish different sensory stimuli. But we don't use it.

Then get into the habit of closing your eyes and smelling nature, things and people (in the latter case, be careful not to go crazy!), and you will be able to provoke real "synaptic explosions" in your brain. mental activation.

7. Brainstorm

Take any activity, simple and obvious, such as opening a bottle. And then try to describe at least 20 different ways of doing it. Exhausting the simplest, such as taking a corkscrew and opening it, you will quickly move on to the more "creative" ones: for example, building a time machine and sending the bottle into the future, where they will open it with telekinesis.

Or send a ladybug to the gym to train, then put it in the cap through a small hole and have it taken it out by pushing from inside (real examples taken from some workshops).

Does it seem stupid to you?

Maybe that's the benefit. By doing the exercise, the brain will start resisting; little by little, it will go to a little used area, the one in which the "suspension of disbelief" is activated. In this way your mind will be able to work without the constraints that normally derive from consistency and logic.

In short, the brain loses its inhibitions, and in addition to giving birth to a lot of bullshit it will be able to increase its ability to churn out creative and effective solutions. To train the mind with this exercise, it is essential that the brain understands the task assigned to it. Otherwise it will not be able to go beyond fifteen theoretical solutions.

Remember that this is not about really opening the bottle, but about temporarily suppressing critical thinking in order to produce as many brain images as possible around a given theme.

8.   Do mental speed exercises

train the mind to "go fast"

Try these exercises to train your mind and with which you can test:

- visual memory
- memory for words
- memory for numbers
- time of reaction to the stimulus.

See, the great thing about forcing your brain to do things quickly is that you naturally focus more. And concentration makes you use your mental abilities better. It is for this reason, for example, that in fast reading, within certain limits, the comprehension of the text increases instead of decreasing.

9. Exercise

When I graduated from medical school, it was thought that new neurons could not grow. Instead, it seems that this is not the case, and that neurogenesis is in fact possible even at a relatively old age. In particular, there are a number of studies that demonstrate neuronal growth within the hippocampus. A deep brain structure involved in memorization processes.

10. Do the Di Caprio in Inception

In the (super cool!) film, Inception, the protagonists build entire imaginary worlds, into which they move after being immersed in a deep sleep. The concept is interesting, and it reminds me of the construction of memory palaces: mental structures that I build in long-term memory thanks to the loci technique, and to which I then link short-term information to remember them.

The effort to construct precise and detailed mental images in our mind, both of things we have seen and of imaginary things, is a very powerful stimulus for the brain, and a skill that is refined and perfected over time. Also, if you know and use memory techniques, you can train yourself by building mental palaces that you will need to memorize information later.

11. Remember things from your past

This is a complete exercise that stimulates concentration, memory areas and creativity at the same time.

Memorizing is different from remembering: the first is in fact the process through which you fix information in your memory; the second is the process by which you retrieve them after having memorized them.

Remembering is itself a form of thinking, but different from logical thinking or reasoning. In fact, when you think about something, for many reasons your brain has become accustomed to using processes connected especially with verbalization.

But when you remember, your brain carries out processes connected mainly with visualization.

In broad terms, that is, we reason with words and remember with images.

Being able to bring visualization into reasoning can give your mind a lot of extra fuel, and we'll see why in the next exercise.

12. Solve "visual" riddles

Have you ever wondered why in many war films there are meetings of generals in front of a model of the terrain, complete with lead soldiers and tanks lined up?

The fact is that strategic reasoning needs to "see" things to be more effective. For example, try to solve this riddle:

"A farmer wants to carry a fox, a goose and a sack of seeds from one side of a river to the other. However, with his boat he can only carry one thing at a time. But if he leaves the fox alone with the goose, the fox eats it. And if he leaves the goose alone with the seeds, the goose eats the seeds. How then does he carry the three from one top to the other? "

Solution:

The first step can only be to bring the goose from bank A to bank B: if it brought the seeds, in fact, the fox and goose would remain on bank A, with the first eating the second.

And if he brought the fox, there would remain goose and seeds together, with the goose eating them.

On the second journey he can carry both the fox and the seeds from one bank to the other. But in any case, he will have to bring the goose back (to avoid the fox / goose or goose / seed combinations).

There are therefore two scenarios:

If he takes the fox from A to B he must bring the goose back to A, take the seeds, bring them to B, go back, take the goose back and bring it back to B.

If instead he brings the seeds to B, he brings the goose back to side A, takes the fox, takes it to B, goes back to A, takes the goose and brings it to B.

Like most problems that require planning in the correct order of a series of actions to be solved (just like in strategic sciences), this riddle is solved more easily only if you are able to accurately visualize the various scenarios. alternative.

Reflections on exercises to train the mind

The exercises that I have proposed to you are, in the description, quite different from each other. But there are some rules that are repeated often and make them similar:

Mental visualization is a powerful stimulus for memory, creativity and problem solving

The senses other than sight must be stimulated more than you usually do, because you use them little and badly

Sight must be stimulated, but in a different way than usual, that is, by changing the perspective

Positive emotional contents (play, relaxation, good memories) are, for the mind, like a nice regenerating massage.

In short, the brain, to increase its level of activation, seems to need to break the monotony with which it interprets and interacts with reality, using new points of view and giving things new and pleasant emotional contents.

And then it doesn't get bored and finds interest in things and self-confidence. As well as its owner.

The greatest benefit of doing these exercises in my opinion is that they remind us that we have a brain and give us the awareness of its different abilities and possibilities. And training the mind often means, after all, only using parts of it that we have forgotten we have.

What Happens to Your Brain After 8 Weeks of Mindfulness Meditation?

We spend most of our life without noticing what happens one meter from our nose. It's not just the iPhone's fault: our mind organizes the little attention we have by distributing it according to the needs and desires we feel.

However, since these needs are for the most part induced by the society to which we belong and by the ecosystem in which we grew up, most of the time we feel unsatisfied and we are moved to action to solve this problem.

To live intentionally we need to de-prioritize our needs and wants

This allows us to remove the feeling of chronic dissatisfaction that keeps us in that busy state condemned by Socrates. The solution or at least one possible solution, and one that has worked for me is mindfulness. Simply put, focus on the here and now.

Mindfulness meditation is an ancient practice that we should rediscover, for the well-being of our physical health and mental balance. Mindfulness implies full attention, which means that our mind is in a relaxed but alert state, perfectly attuned to the "here and now".

But what does Mindfulness practically consist of?

Mindfulness is, in practice, a form of meditation, therefore it requires time, energy, determination, steadfastness and discipline. From the point of view of mental processes, it takes the form of paying attention, in the present moment, to four elements:

- ✓ your body
- ✓ their own sensory perceptions (physiological, physical and psychological belonging to the broad domains of pleasant, unpleasant, mixed and neutral)
- ✓ mental formations (e.g. anger, pain or compassion)
- ✓ the objects of the mind (every mental formation has an object, one is angry with someone and for something etc...).

The observation of these elements of one's subjective experience takes place in a state of authentic non-reactive calm, in which one accepts what is observed for what it is, allowing changes to occur naturally, without hindering or promoting them and avoiding the usual resistance or the usual judgment that cause further suffering.

Through mindfulness, full awareness and active presence are promoted

Thanks to all this, our senses are amplified but we get rid of the need to intervene and judge what we are experiencing. We learn to flow. Therefore, practicing transcendental meditation systematically produces very positive changes in our daily life, in the way we relate to others, in which we deal with setbacks and also in the way we relate to ourselves.

"The inner changes generated by mindfulness meditation are so powerful that many psychologists have included it in their arsenal of therapeutic techniques"

In fact, a recent study conducted at the University of Oxford with 1258 patients concluded that "mindfulness therapy is as effective as antidepressants, but does not have the same side effects". These researchers also found that mindfulness is particularly effective in people suffering from recurring depression and, more interestingly, that it is very effective in preventing it.

Now a group of researchers from the Netherlands has gone a step further by showing that mindfulness meditation not only works on a psychological level, but also causes changes in the brain.

"There is a space between the stimulus
and the response. In that space is our power to
choose the answer. In our answers lies our ability to
grow and our freedom "

VIKTOR FRANKL

A more connected, relaxed and attentive brain

These neuroscientists have conducted a systematic review of all the studies done to date on mindfulness meditation, to evaluate how this practice can change the brain in just 8 weeks.

They based their research on 30 previous studies that analyzed the functional and structural changes that occur in the brain when people start practicing meditation.

It turned out that the studies reported changes both in the level of activity as well as in the volume and degree of neuronal connectivity in different areas of the brain:

- ✓ Prefrontal cortex, an area involved in decision making and emotional regulation
- ✓ The amygdala, a structure that acts as a protection against the dangers of the environment and modulates emotional reactions
- ✓ The hippocampus, a structure that plays a key role in learning and memory
- ✓ The insula, a structure related to body representation, which also allows you to become aware of emotions, feelings and desires
- ✓ The anterior cingulate cortex, a very important area not only involved in the regulation of heart rate and blood pressure, but also in decision-making and empathy.

The changes found in the brain coincide with other experiments, in which it was found that meditation helps regulate our emotional state, make better decisions, improve memory and amplify concentration.

In fact, researchers from Harvard University and Justus Liebig-University have delved into this practice to understand its action in the brain.

They thus concluded that mindfulness meditation works through some fundamental aspects:

1. It helps people have more control over their mind, for example by helping them to develop full attention and ignore distractions.

2. It facilitates a greater awareness of one's body, allowing people to perceive the small signals sent by the body and thus be able to counteract stress before it grows too much.

3. Stimulates emotional self-control, particularly the ability to deal with "negative" or unpleasant emotions, making people use their experiences more effectively.

4. Change the perception of one's "me" as people abandon the idea that their personality is permanent and unchanging, which has a powerful therapeutic effect and promotes compassion for oneself.

However, perhaps most interesting is that these changes occur after only 8 weeks of systematic practice, which means that you don't need to lock yourself up in a Buddhist monastery to get all these benefits, you just need to be constant. In fact, it takes so little to transform you into a conscious person.

These changes can be seen in:

- ✓ a greater ability to master life's difficult situations
- ✓ greater power to manage conflicts and ordinary and extraordinary problems
- ✓ an increase in acceptance and patience towards one's own state of illness or psychological and physical infirmities
- ✓ a new capacity of the mind to replace destructive emotions, which lead to anxiety and depression, with more constructive ways of being, which promote equanimity, love and wisdom.

Is mindful meditation for everyone?

Despite the multiple benefits of mindful meditation some people may not feel comfortable with this practice. In fact, a study from the early 1990s indicated that during the first few weeks of practice some people may suffer from loss of motivation or panic attacks.

Another, more recent study done at the University of Washington looked at cases in which this type of meditation was linked with increased anxiety, depersonalization and headaches. Why?

The problem is that mindfulness meditation involves a deep exploration of our "inner space", and not all people are psychologically prepared for this. Finding yourself face to face with the suffering and resentment accumulated over the years, body tensions, critical thoughts and all those things hidden from your conscience, can be devastating.

The time has come to put things right and you can do it through full self-awareness.

HOW, WHERE AND WHEN

Of utmost importance is constant, hopefully daily practice. There is no ideal time, the only recommendation is not to meditate in the two hours after meals because the relaxation response evoked by the practice interferes with the digestive processes and vice versa. A few minutes a day are enough to start, preferably at the same time of the day in order to establish a habit that favors daily practice.

One can meditate anywhere, even in the midst of confusion. In the early stages it is advisable to choose a quiet environment that does not distract us too much.

It can help the breathing exercises to handle negative emotions.

A specific posture is not necessary, the important thing is to be comfortable and take a position that can be maintained for the entire duration of the meditation and that allows you to breathe without fatigue. Sitting, lying down or in yoga positions ... the choice is yours.

Final remarks

In summary: meditating leads us to mindfulness, and this allows us to expand the space in which to seek answers to the accidents of life, learning to act on what we can control and accepting what we can do nothing about. Thus, erasing that state of chronic dissatisfaction in which we are stuck.

The Vagus Nerve – Senses and Shapes Your Health

A "Mindfulness Yoga" perspective

The vagus nerve is the longest nerve in the human body, it starts from the lowest section of the brain, called the brain stem, from the medulla oblongata just behind the ears, from there it goes down the two sides of the neck, along the chest and to the abdomen.

The term "vago" comes from the Latin word "vagus", which means "vagabond", "wandering". Probably, doctors coined this name in reference to the long and intricate path that the vagus nerve takes within the human body.

In its course towards the abdomen, it establishes numerous innervations: with the external auditory canal, with the pharynx, larynx and trachea, with the lungs, heart, stomach and intestines. It connects the brain to the nerves involved in speech, eye contact and facial expressions.

What it is for / What it does

80-90% of the nerve fibers of the vagus nerve are dedicated to informing the brain of what is happening in the viscera, in particular in the digestive organs but more generally its functions are to:

INFORM the brain of what is happening (sensory function)

PERFORM actions (motor function)

An indicator of resilience

Have you ever noticed that a segment of the population is made up of people whose body, brain and mind are more stable and robust in all kinds of situations? These people are not troubled by wealth or adversity, and they manage to maintain their equanimity in conditions of excitement, enthusiasm, momentum or in boring, tragic and rational moments. These individuals tend to be healthier and more resilient and are classified as "high vagal tone" people. These people are more resistant to stress and can easily move from an excited to a relaxed state and back without being overly upset. These individuals not only have ease in handling stressful situations, but tend to have excellent stamina and are generally healthier.

Conversely, people with low vagal tone are more sensitive to stress and can easily fall prey to the disease. They tend to have difficult digestion and difficulty managing emotions. Additionally, people with low vagal tone are easily alarmed and frequently suffer from physical, mental, and emotional disturbances. Low vagal tone correlates with health conditions such as depression, anxiety, chronic stress, and pain.

A higher vagal tone is related to physical and psychological well-being

Low vagal tone is linked to inflammation, negative moods, loneliness, and heart attacks

So, what exactly is vagal tone? Vagal tone defines the functional state of the vagus nerve and is its degree of activity within the parasympathetic nervous system. Furthermore, the immune capacity and resilience of an individual directly depends on the activity of the vagal nerve.

Low vagal tone is associated with a number of health risks, while people with high vagal tone are not only healthier, but also socially and psychologically stronger, able to focus better and remember things, happier and with less likely to be depressed, more empathetic, and more likely to have close friendships.

Studies on twins show that vagal tone is genetically predetermined, some people are born luckier than others. But low vagal tone is more common in people with certain lifestyles, such as those who do little exercise, for example.

How does all this have to do with yoga?

Several research studies suggest that Yoga practices such as Pranayama (breathing techniques) Pratyahara (withdrawal of the senses) and Asanas (postures), can significantly increase vagal tone and improve symptoms of various conditions, including anxiety and depression.

Why is it so important?

Operating far below the level of our conscious minds, the vagus nerve is a vital nerve to keep our body healthy.

Here's why it's so important:

It helps improve mood

Researchers have shown that vagus nerve stimulation can be an effective chronic depression treatment for those unresponsive to conventional treatments.

It is essential in managing fear

Research has shown that healthy functioning of the vagus nerve helps us recover from stressful situations and overcome fear-induced conditioning.

It plays a role in learning and memory

A scientific study has shown that a low vagal tone causes greater difficulty in reconnecting an environment previously experienced as "dangerous" with a new "safe" and neutral situation.

Helps reduce inflammation

Stimulation of the vagus nerve reduces the overproduction of TNF (an inflammatory protein, tumor necrosis factor) that causes chronic inflammation.

It has deep control over heart rate and blood pressure

Patients with heart failure tend to have a weakly active vagus nerve.

It regulates the muscle movement necessary for you to breathe

The brain communicates with the diaphragm via the vagus nerve which releases a neurotransmitter, acetylcholine, to allow breathing. If the vagus nerve stopped releasing acetylcholine, we would stop breathing.

It is involved in the balance between the sympathetic and parasympathetic systems

When the brain triggers parasympathetic activation, the vagus nerve carries messages to the heart (by decreasing heart rate and blood pressure), to the lungs (constriction of the respiratory passages), to all organs of the digestive system (to increase motility and blood flow to the digestive tract, to promote defecation), to the kidneys and bladder (to promote urination), and to the reproductive organs (to promote sexual arousal).

Disorders of Childhood: Anxieties, Phobias and Behavioral Changes

Children represent a fascinating and mysterious world. It's hard not to be amazed at their progress, their abilities and their vitality. It is therefore particularly difficult for parents and caregivers to be confronted with children with problems. You don't know what to do, worry and feel guilty. In this dossier we try to understand some aspects of the child's development and to recognize the problems that may arise. We start with the language: the child begins to pronounce the first words in the first year of life, at a year and a half the first two-word sentences and within another two years he will learn a rich vocabulary and articulate very complex sentences. The changes in the child's behavior are then explained (lying, theft and flight) and finally the anxieties and phobias, from obsessive compulsive disorder to panic disorder, mostly the same disorders that occur in the adult population.

Anxiety and phobias

Children's anxiety disorders are mostly the same as those found in the adult population. From obsessive compulsive disorder to generalized anxiety disorder, from panic disorder to agoraphobia, from specific phobia to social phobia, up to anxiety due to a medical condition. The only anxiety disorder that has been recognized as specific to childhood is separation anxiety disorder.

Diffusion

Studies on the prevalence of anxiety disorders have shown that in a fairly wide age range (between 4 and 20 years) which included children and adolescents, anxiety disorders were present individually or together in 8-12% of the population. These data place anxiety disorders as the most frequent ailments among children. However, alongside this widespread diffusion, these disorders are rarely treated. Regarding obsessive- compulsive disorder, a study showed that its prevalence was one in 200 children. Separation anxiety disorder is more common in younger children, generalized anxiety disorder in older children and panic usually does not occur before puberty. As for the differences between the sexes, it seems that males are prevalent in childhood disorders, while females are prevalent in puberty and adolescence.

Demonstrations

It is difficult to talk about obsessive-compulsive disorder before puberty, if not adolescence. Children mostly manifest so-called rituals, much more rarely obsessive ideas. Obsessive behaviors have two sides: one at the level of thought characterized by obsessions, the other at the level of actions, characterized by rituals and compulsions. Obsessions are ideas from which one cannot get rid of and which give feelings of extreme discomfort while the ritual can be considered as a protracted repetition of generally verification behaviors (check if things are in their place). Finally, compulsion is a feeling characterized by the compulsion to make a gesture. Rituals are a way to control the child's distress. Among these, the most frequent are the rituals related to falling asleep (a moment of particular anguish). In such cases, parents can try to indulge the child by telling a story that the child wants to hear and reassuring him, even letting him put certain objects where he wants. Such behavior will likely be able to contain the child's distress, gradually allowing him to no longer feel the need for the rituals to feel safe. Different is the case in which these children come from a family background with obsessive characteristics, in which case, these behaviors of the child will probably be favored. This turns out to be a great risk factor for the emergence of an obsessive organization.

Generalized anxiety disorder is characterized by a painful feeling of worry and anxious anticipation about possible terrifying events that could happen. There are depressive ideas with feelings of guilt related to the present and the past, the need for reassurance and closeness, extreme fear of possible disastrous future events, as well as irritable mood, anger and complaints. It is probable that in particular moments of difficulty (such as real separations even on holidays, or school insertion) the most acute crises of anguish: panic attacks.

Panic attacks can occur singly or become part of panic disorders, if they are recurrent and followed by periods of intense worry about a repetition of the attack and its consequences. They can occur within the disorder with or without agoraphobia which we will describe later. Panic attacks are characterized by the presence of intense fear associated with somatic, motor, vasomotor, neurological and psychic symptoms that develop suddenly and rapidly, such as: changes in heart rate, sweating, tremors, dizziness, nausea, fear of dying or going crazy, etc. Only parents can calm these crises, which occur more on the somatic side the younger the child is. Later, in older children, there may be the transition to the act with anger, destructiveness and flight. In these cases, a firm but benevolent attitude is essential to calm and be able to contain these crises of anguish.

Agoraphobia represents anxiety related to being in places from which it would not be easy to leave or get help. Generally, the places that arouse these fears are places where you find yourself alone and away from home, such as crowded places or public or private means of transport. This fear involves the avoidance of anxious places.

Separation anxiety manifests itself with fear, worries, nightmares and malaise on the occasion of separations from attachment figures or simply the idea of such separations. The fear is that something may happen to them or that some dramatic event will result in the separation of family members. This fear manifests itself in the difficulty or inability for the child to sleep alone, go to sleep at the home of relatives or friends, carry out normal school or recreational activities. To make a diagnosis, separation anxiety must have lasted for at least 4 weeks. An early onset form is recognized, before 6 years of age.

Phobias are unjustified fears related to events or objects, the contact of which causes a strong anxiety reaction. Some phobias have already been described (such as agoraphobia) and in all of them there are counterphobic attitudes of avoidance and escape (for example, staying indoors).

A specific phobia refers to fears related to objects or situations such as animals, darkness, water, while social phobia is related to the fear of being in social situations in which one could be exposed to the observation and judgment of others. The most classic example of social phobia in children is the school phobia. Phobias have obvious secondary benefits such as being in close contact with parents and having their attention. The development and evolution of phobias are closely linked to the family environment. There are often family phobic situations, for example the fear of dogs: terrified parents will, in all likelihood, transmit their fear to the child. In a reassuring family environment, but not complicit (an excessive understanding of the phobias could reinforce the behavior) it is easy for the phobias to resolve around 7-8 years old. It is also essential to consider that fears are a practically constant aspect in growth, they must make parents worry when they are so pervasive as to distress the child and prevent him from carrying out his daily life in a peaceful way.

Treatments

It is important to treat anxiety disorders, as they, when moderate or severe, rarely undergo spontaneous remission and are often replaced by other disorders, usually other anxiety or depressive syndromes.

Psychodynamic and systemic therapy and cognitive behavioral therapies are often used among psychotherapies. Prescribed drugs are usually SSRI (selective serotonin reuptake inhibitors) antidepressants, benzodiazepines and beta-blockers. It seems that the disorder that responds best to antidepressants is obsessive-compulsive disorder.

Behavioral alterations

The behavioral alterations that will be described below, namely lying, theft and flight, have the common characteristic of being closely related to the socialization process and its possible deviations. These are behaviors that, if isolated or rare, do not have a pathological significance, whereas this is assumed in cases in which they are continuously repeated over time.

The lie

Lying is the conscious alteration of the truth. It can be considered as a new possibility for the child linked to the acquisition of language. If, in fact, language allows you to describe what is not present, then language can also be used to modify what you want to communicate. The child not only discovers that he cannot say everything, but that he can also make things up. Clearly, in order to talk about the alteration of reality, it is necessary to understand when the child understands the distinction between fantasy and reality, between true and false. Generally, the child is considered to consolidate these skills around the age of six or seven. Lying can be a way to maintain a perfect self-image, or to establish a boundary between oneself and parents. If, on the one hand, lying can enslave useful purposes, of conquest and independence, on the other, the child soon learns that telling the truth means respecting social needs and obtaining the esteem of others. The truth will then be used to gratify the parents and to increase self-esteem, while the lie will maintain an illusion of perfection, which will only lower self-esteem.

There are three main types of lying:

- **the utilitarian lie**
- **the compensatory lie**
- **mythomania.**

The utilitarian lie is the one closest to the lie used by adults: lying to avoid or get something. The fact that lies remain isolated facts or become a mode of communication is closely connected to the behavior and reaction of parents. On the one hand, it will be important not to shame the child and not to have an overly moralizing attitude. In fact, in this case the terrified child may be tempted to lie again to try to get by or get an idea of himself as a bad child, who cannot deserve the esteem of the parents, with the consequence that the child will tend to behave as the parents expect: as a bad child. On the other hand, a lax or gullible attitude risk paving the way for a more frequent use of lies, to get by in various circumstances. Perhaps, however, the most important element that determines subsequent behaviors is the sincerity of the parents themselves. Being honest allows you to give the child an idea of reliability and solidity. A constructive attitude will involve detecting the child's lie without raging on him and giving him the feeling that having done a "mean" does not mean being a bad child.

Compensatory lying is used by the child to obtain an image that he deems unattainable and desirable. The child can invent anything, he can say that he is the son of a king, that he lives in a castle, that he has a horse. Often children invent characters with which they converse. This behavior is not worrying until the age of 6, after which it can be an indication of immaturity, alterations and uncertainties in identification and self-awareness.

Mythomania represents the extreme degree of compensatory lying. It is a tendency to the limit between the voluntary and the involuntary. In young children it can be considered almost physiological, but in general mythomania, being an extreme manifestation, occurs in contexts of severe affective deprivation, in children who do not have one or both parents, who have never known them, and / or with severe identification disorders.

Theft

Theft is the most frequent behavioral alteration and accounts for approximately 70 percent of juvenile delinquent conduct. It is committed much more frequently by males than females. To be able to talk about theft it is necessary that the child has the notion of "property", and that he has also developed the notion of "good" and "evil". The small child, in fact, considers everything as his and only from the age of six or seven can he not only understand that he is appropriating something not his own, but also that this is wrong. Different ages are characterized by different types of theft, there is not necessarily a consequential relationship between a child who steals and the fact that he becomes a thief when he grows up. Children start stealing from home, mostly things they want, then from home they move on to busy environments such as school or shops. It is a different theft from the previous one, in fact it is committed not so much for the interest in the object, as to commit the act of theft. Guilt is often not present in younger children, while it characterizes older ones. This explains why stolen items are often left in visible places, as if to provoke punishment. In older children, theft often takes on a meaning within the group, revealing more worrying characteristics.

The family context of the child who commits thefts is almost all of the time a context of absence, of real or emotional deficiencies, of extremes characterized by maximum rigor or complete laxity. Many authors have pointed out that the child who steals is as if trying to regain possession of something that belongs to him by right: the mother and her affection. It is essential to grasp this aspect and try to support the child in his search for answers and affection. Theft can be one of the first steps on the road to delinquency, it is aimed at obtaining material benefits and often the sense of guilt is absent. It is not uncommon for it to be part of an initiation rite for entering a group (mostly of a deviant type).

Escape

In order to talk about escape, that is, the abandonment of the place where the child should be, it is necessary to identify the moment in which the child is aware of his home. Escape is not loss. For this reason, we can speak of escape from the age of six or seven. The escape has a duration that can vary from a few hours to a few days. In young children, escapes are mostly motivated by the desire to reach a place or loved ones (such as a parent or grandparents) or to escape from a feared or detested place. Most of the time the child wanders around the house and aims to be found. There are no personality characteristics of fugitives. We often observe the escape in children who have gone through many separations and detachments, with no one to help them process them, (children in conflicting institutions or families). Another frequent escape is the flight from school. This occurs mainly in children who have difficulty succeeding, in anxious children or those with a school phobia. At other times, the escape is part of a psychopathic picture. Most of the time these episodes end, either because the family notices them, or because the child is no longer able to tolerate the burden of distress and confesses. Don't underestimate the secondary benefits a child can get from seeing angry and, above all, worried parents. It is important to try to understand the discomfort that the child experiences to prevent the escape conduct from being used whenever the child desires affection and consideration in the minds of the parents.

Conclusion

The 8 benefits of Resilience

Let's see what the 8 benefits of resilience are and why cultivating it helps us manage this historical moment full of complexity and change.

One of the characteristics useful for achieving great goals is the ability to return to our challenges again and again: and personal and work lives are full of challenges and difficulties, sometimes unexpected. To be successful we must embrace our inner warrior and find our resilient ability. Resilience is our ability to draw energy from within to move forward, to continue to have hope.

Hope, one of the 10 positive emotions Fredrickson identified, is the magical emotion that remembers our dream, why we are doing what we are doing and the reasons we started. Hope is the foundation of resilience. It is that very powerful and famous pot of gold that we will find at the end of our story, which makes the suffering we experience to get there worth it.

1. Sense of community

There is no question: we are more resilient when we have supportive relationships to turn to. Being resilient is a capacity that develops in situations of suffering, but it is not linked only to the individual and connects well with the community, which supports us in being more resilient.

Resilience requires sharing, even if it is a two-way sharing. The best scenario is to have a community that is diverse in experience, age, perspectives, talents, abilities and points of view.

These differences help us be more resilient. Having a sense of community teaches us to look outward and see a greatness that exists beyond our individual desires. We are able to see that we can bring about such a significant change, which makes individual adversity interesting as well.

2.   Nothing is insurmountable

We cannot allow others to say "No" to us. We must hold the deep conviction that nothing is insurmountable. There is always more than one way to climb the same mountain. Resilience isn't just about fighting and surviving, it's about being resourceful enough to thrive. We need to be able to turn every "No" into a "forward to the next", make the decision to dig deep and do what we think is insurmountable.

Once we see that we can do what we thought impossible, we are better prepared for the new challenges that we will surely tackle with determination. Resilience requires a certain stubbornness to do what we set out to do, regardless of adversity.

3. Change is a constant

Change and challenge are fundamental for the development of who we are and are a constant. The way we manage change is a sign of our adaptability and resilience.

To be resilient, we need to be flexible in the face of changes that arise. As we face a challenge, each of us has the right and responsibility to examine the roads that precede us and those we have already traveled. As we take stock of where we are now, however, we also have the right to abandon all negative paths, without feeling ashamed or embarrassed, and take another direction. To be resilient, we must be wise enough to understand that when we cannot change our circumstances, we must change ourselves.

4. Stick to your dream

Entrepreneurs are often told to find their "why" (Simon Sinek's book, 'Starting from the why' is beautiful in this regard), but few know that the origins of this advice are born from Viktor Frankl's search for meaning, in his remarkable memoir of survivors of the Auschwitz extermination camp. Frankl realized in Auschwitz that what differentiated the survivors from those who had died was a combination of luck and a strong reason to live. In fact, Frankl wrote: "When a man knows the 'why' of his existence, he will be able to endure any 'how'".

The responsibility we carry in life is always towards others, because love, more than success or wealth, gives us the deepest and most significant reason to move forward. Our "why" is what motivates us to hold onto our dreams. Happiness, resilience and motivation increase enormously when we have something to look forward to, a goal; therefore, it is imperative to stay focused on our bigger picture when facing difficulties. In this way, happiness and success are not the goal of our journey, but rather the side effect of it.

5. Cultivate your mind by reading stories of change

Go in search of other people's successes. When we are in the midst of our most difficult times, it is essential to find stories of those who have survived experiences similar to ours. Through their stories we find hope, new perspectives and new ways to face our trials.

We can make use of great poetry, meaningful stories, music and movies. All these resources will inspire us to find our own purpose. Reading feeds our mind and develops our wisdom. Through reading, we grow our education and fortitude to align with the challenges our journey requires. When we feed our minds, we feed our spirits. Reading helps build our resilience because it fills our minds with information that inspires us to do.

6. Keep moving

To keep moving we need to be strong. Resilience isn't limited to just surviving the depths and terrors of routine. It also means keeping a heart full of hope, believing in the magic of this universe, and never losing a sense of humor. If we take ourselves too seriously, we burn ourselves out. We must strive to be as light as possible. Pressure kills desire. Movement is inspired by desire, joy and the ability to remain strong in our beliefs. To keep moving we need to have backbone, the will and the deep commitment to keep taking the next step towards our goal.

7. Self-discovery

It is normal to get down when we are tested. We may lose faith in ourselves, or go through times when we feel we are doing everything wrong. The difficulties we face in life and work are essential to our success. It is from our suffering that we recognize our depth, resilience and wisdom. We come to discover the true meaning behind who we are and what we are made of. The challenge leads us to the door of our personal and professional transcendence. Through self-discovery, we find clarity. We are able to discover, recognize and manage our blind spots. We learn to remove our barriers, challenging old beliefs, analysis and all the false assumptions we can stand. We find that we don't need to change ourselves, but focus on our improvement.

8. Love yourself

When we love ourselves, we laugh more, smile and are more resilient. We must be authentic and not hide what we are from others. Authenticity is what creates and deepens the bonds.

When we love ourselves, we have that undeniable resilience, which naturally elevates the spirits of others as well. It is important to love and recognize others, give them hope and breathe goodness into them. When we feel valued, we are much more likely to have our say and speak out for our own integrity and that of others against negativity.

Resilience helps us develop a voice that competes with other people's judgments.

Resilience gives us the stamina to get through our toughest times. It is important to have community support and individual tenacity to never give up on our aspirations. We must constantly remind ourselves that we are something miraculous; the true wonders of the world. Things will not always go the right way, so we need to look within, hold on to our visions and adapt to the changes we face.

We must never underestimate who we are and what we can do for others.

To be resilient, we need to appreciate all people. Above all, we must never take "No" for an answer. If we do, we allow another to determine our destiny. We must be able to determine our worth, our destiny.